WHAT WOULD JESUS DO?

WHAT WOULD JESUS DO?

A FAMILY DEVOTIONAL FOR PRETEENS AND PARENTS

CONVERSATION STARTERS ON LIFE, LOVE, AND FAITH

Lucy Rycroft

Z Faith Kids • New York

Z Faith Kids
An imprint of Zeitgeist™
A division of Penguin Random House LLC
1745 Broadway, New York, NY 10019
zeitgeistpublishing.com
penguinrandomhouse.com

ISBN: 9798217151059
Ebook ISBN: 9798217151042

Printed in the United States of America
1st Printing

Illustrations © by Anastasiia Hevko/Shutterstock.com
Book design by Aimee Fleck
Author photograph © by Joy Photography (Lucy Baines)
Edited by Kim Suarez

The authorized representative in the EU for product safety and compliance is Penguin Random House Ireland, Morrison Chambers, 32 Nassau Street, Dublin D02 YH68, Ireland.
https://eu-contact.penguin.ie

To my own preteens, Zac and Ben. Thank you for the energy, laughter, creativity, and fun you bring to our family. And thank you for constantly keeping me on my toes with experiences, scenarios, and questions I'd never considered! This book is for you.

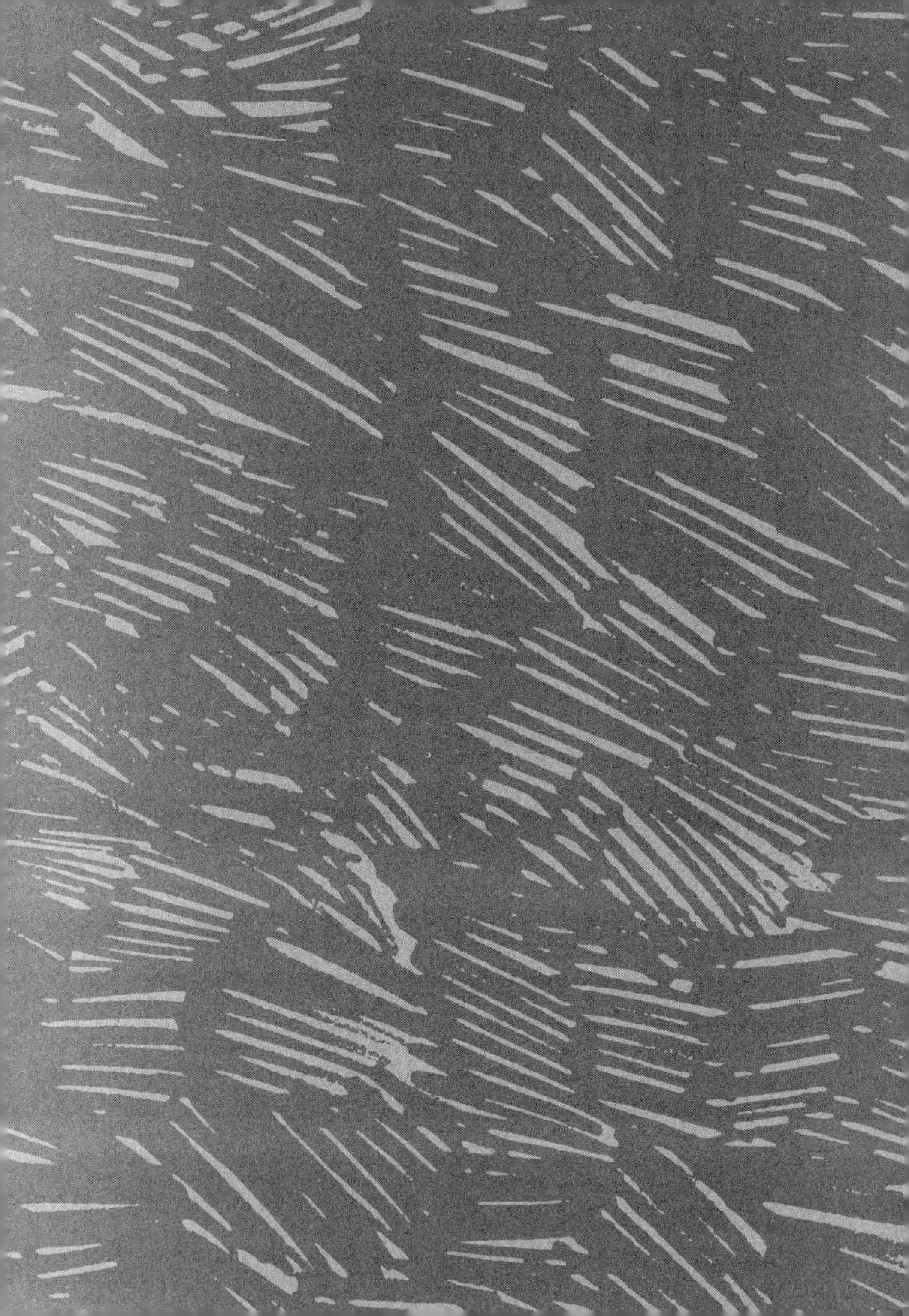

CONTENTS

Introduction 9

How to Use This Book 12

Friendships and Relationships 19
Weeks 1–10

Home and Family 41
Weeks 11–17

School 57
Weeks 18–25

Mental and Emotional Health 75
Weeks 26–34

Technology 95
Weeks 35–39

Puberty and Growing Up 107
Weeks 40–47

Money and Independence 125
Weeks 48–52

Acknowledgments 137

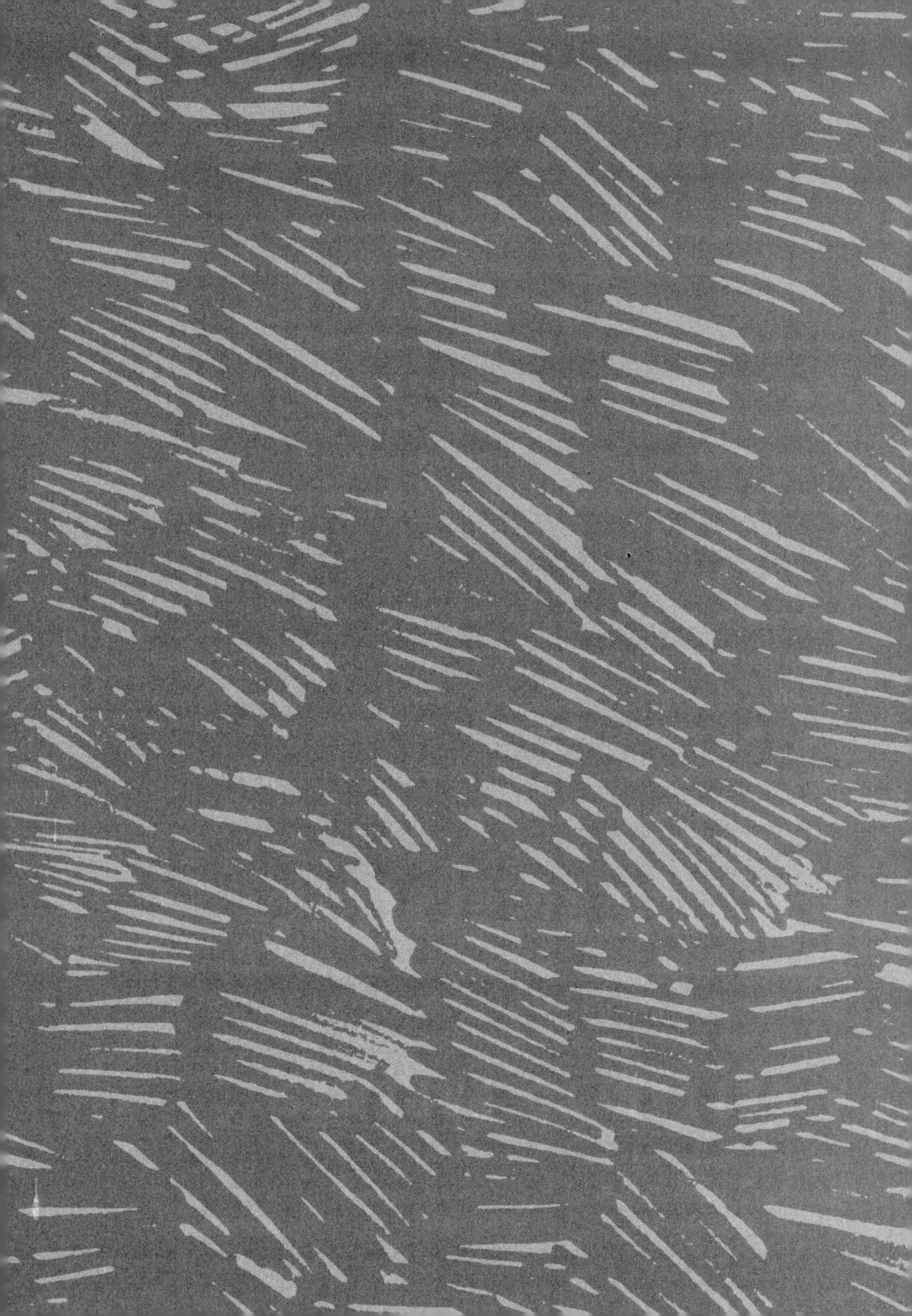

INTRODUCTION

A LETTER TO PARENTS

It probably feels like just a few minutes since your beautiful child was taking their first steps—but here they are, preteens on the cusp of teenagerhood, and your head is spinning with questions:

When did they grow up? Did I make the most of their first few years? How do I parent them through all the friend drama, crushes, mounting homework and tests, and increasing independence of the next few years? Are they turning into responsible individuals? Help!

Unlike us, however, God is not fazed by any parenting season. He created us to develop through childhood and teenagerhood as we do—mood swings and all! None of it is a surprise to him. And his word, the Bible, gives wisdom for all of life's ups and downs.

That's where this devotional comes in.

Our kids are on a journey of discovery with God—testing his word, wondering if it's true. Their bodies, minds, and lives are changing. They're starting to widen their horizons—literally and mentally. They're asking big questions, formulating how they feel about the world around them. They need to know that the God they've learned about in children's Bibles is real, alive, and deeply interested in them and the things that concern them.

This book will help you navigate this new phase of parenting, as you and your child together read devotions that are directed specifically toward preteens. By engaging them directly, your preteen will be encouraged to discover that Jesus's way is the best way in all the ebbs and flows of life. These devotions are intended to be the start—not the end—of a deeper conversation between you and your child, in which you listen to their experiences, bring the Bible's truth and relevance to their situation, and together lift up ongoing concerns to your heavenly Father.

As a mom of two teens and two preteens, as well as a schoolteacher of this age group, I'm all too familiar with the friendship fallouts, phone boundaries, increasing school pressure, first crushes, start of puberty, and all the other joys that this age group has to deal with on a regular basis. While the world has changed a lot since you and I were this age, much of what our kids go through we have experienced ourselves. The insights you offer your child in this season are invaluable—and, when covered in God's word, are powerful to help them navigate the next few years with passion and purpose.

So, enjoy this book! Enjoy that it gives you openers for tricky conversations. Enjoy that it helps you bring God into conversations in a natural way. And enjoy the privilege of talking with your preteen about life and how God is right there with them in it all.

Lucy

HOW TO USE THIS BOOK

What's in This Book

You're holding 52 weeks' worth of encouraging devotions in your hands, each one addressing an issue common to 10-to-12-year-olds.

Please don't feel you have to read from start to finish! Each devotion is standalone, so go ahead and pick whichever issue is relevant to your child. If they've had a fallout with a friend, head to that chapter. If they don't have siblings, you'll want to skip that devotion. If they have no interest in dating, feel free to leave that section until they do!

Each devotion opens with a Bible verse, followed by a short commentary, unlocking the Bible's relevance to the topic. Then five conversation starters explore the topic further. These could even form the basis of devotions on subsequent days if you wish.

Finally, there's a short prayer to help preteens articulate to God what they might be feeling. However, do encourage your child to chat with God naturally too—he doesn't need fancy words!

A Note for Preteens: Understanding God's Word

You may have read a lot of the Bible before—or you may be just beginning. It doesn't matter either way! What matters most is that you've picked up this book and are open to seeing if God has things to say to you that may help as you navigate life. Here are some tips for how to learn to listen to God through his word:

- Use a modern Bible translation. Here, we're using the New Living Translation (NLT), which you can find on biblegateway.com.
- Read the given verse/s slowly, and read them 2–3 times if you can. Allow the meaning to sink in.
- If it's hard to understand, try another translation—maybe The Message (MSG), International Children's Bible (ICB), or Good News Translation (GNT).
- Ask yourself key questions—What does this passage tell me about God, Jesus, or the Holy Spirit? What does this passage tell me about myself? About other people? How does this apply to my life today? This week? This year?
- Talk to God about what you've just read. Tell him what encourages you and what challenges you. Ask him what he wants you to learn from it.
- Talk about the passage with someone else: a parent or guardian, a youth pastor, or a Christian friend. What do they think it means?

A Note for Parents: How to Talk to Your Preteen

I know it's not always easy talking about big issues with kids. We all have areas that are painful or awkward for us to address because of how we were raised or experiences we've had. My prayer is that this book makes it easier for us to develop an open communication culture with our children: one that will underpin our relationship with them through adulthood.

How do we do that? Here are some ideas:

- Think carefully about when to start big conversations. Don't attempt them when your child is overly tired, hungry, or feeling big emotions.
- Consider how to make it a special time for you both. Adding your child's favorite snack or drink will give them positive associations with reading God's word!
- Sometimes it's easier to talk alongside each other rather than face-to-face. Consider pairing your chat with a drive, a walk, or a baking or craft project.
- Ask open-ended questions (the conversation starters are great for this) and listen to your child's answers. Try not to interrupt (this is my personal Achilles' heel!).
- Listen intentionally to your child's thoughts, opinions, and experiences. Ask open-ended questions that seek insight to understand their life better.

- Be careful that your language doesn't accidentally judge or belittle your child, their friends, or their interests. Remember, they are working out who God has made them to be and what he has put them in this world for.
- If you hear an opinion you disagree with, aim to be gentle in your response. You could say, "That's an interesting thought. Another way of looking at it is . . ."

WEEKS
1-10

FRIENDSHIPS AND RELATIONSHIPS

What a good friend looks like

Don't just pretend to love others. Really love them. Hate what is wrong. Hold tightly to what is good. Love each other with genuine affection, and take delight in honoring each other.

ROMANS 12:9-10

Are you a lots-of-friends type person or a one-best-friend person? Maybe you're a bit of a mix—or maybe friendships are something you're struggling with right now.

Friendship isn't always easy, and we can't change other people (how great would that be?!)—but we *can* do something about *our* actions and attitude.

In this passage, Paul (the author of Romans) shares three ways we can be good friends:

Love: *"Don't just pretend to love others. Really love them."* This isn't sappy, romantic love—this is real, gutsy love: showing kindness to our friends, considering their needs, wanting the best for them, and forgiving them when they mess up.

Integrity: *"Hate what is wrong. Hold tightly to what is good."* Strong friendships focus on what is good and true. They don't pay attention to gossip or rumors.

Encouragement: *"Take delight in honoring each other."* Respect who God has made our friends to be, encouraging them, and cheering them on.

Wow, this is quite a list!

The good news is that we don't have to simply "try" and be all these things. God is perfect in all of these areas and, through his Holy Spirit, equips us with everything we need to be a good friend.

Whether friendships are happening right now or not, we can pray for these qualities and look for opportunities to practice them with those we meet.

CONVERSATION STARTERS

- If Jesus lived in your neighborhood as a kid, what kind of a friend do you think he'd be?
- Can you think of a friend who is really loving? One who is really honest? And one who is really encouraging?
- Read 1 Corinthians 13, which talks about love. Which of the qualities mentioned are you good at? Which ones could you ask God to grow in you?
- Reflect even more by taking a look at John 15:12–17. How does it make you feel that Jesus calls you his friend?

PRAYER

Dear Jesus, thank you for the gift of friendship, especially for my friends ___________ (name them here). Please help me grow in the things that will make me a good friend to them. And thank you most of all for inviting me to be your friend too. Amen.

When a friend isn't a friend anymore . . .

"Love your enemies! Do good to those who hate you. Bless those who curse you. Pray for those who hurt you."

LUKE 6:27-28

Have you ever had a friend turn their back on you? It really hurts.

Many of Jesus's followers lost friends because they chose to follow Jesus. So Jesus gives them some wisdom. But it doesn't sound very wise . . .

I mean—when someone hurts us, we want to hate them, not love them!

If someone is unkind, we want to wish them harm, not good!

When a "friend" betrays us, we want to curse them, not bless them!

And what's this about *praying* for those who have hurt us? Why waste my prayers on them? Doesn't Jesus know what betrayal feels like?

Actually, yes. Jesus was betrayed by a close friend, mocked by those who had previously celebrated him, and had his best friend deny being friends with him. As betrayals go, I think that's pretty bad.

Yet what was his response? Did he say, "Uh . . . sorry, guys. That thing I said about loving your enemies—maybe I was asking too much after all"?

No! Even while in excruciating pain on the cross, Jesus asked God to *forgive* his enemies.

Jesus doesn't tell us to do stuff he doesn't do himself. In every word and action, he models love, goodness, and forgiveness. He knows how it feels when someone hurts us. So, when we ask him, he gives us the strength to do the impossible: love, do good, bless, and pray for those who hurt us.

CONVERSATION STARTERS

- If Jesus were in your class/homeschool group/sports team/other activity, how do you think he would show love and do good?
- Have you had the experience of a friend betraying you? How did/does it feel?
- What might it look like to love them and do good to them? Try to picture this, and talk about how it might play out.
- Read Luke 23:34-38. How many different "betrayal" actions can you count in these verses? How do you think Jesus was able to pray for those who were hurting him?
- Although it might feel better to curse the person who has hurt us, this does not lead to peace. However, praying for them really does help heal our hearts toward them. Why not pray for them now? You could use the blessing in Numbers 6:24–26 as your guide.

PRAYER

Lord Jesus, you were so brave to pray for your enemies on the cross. I've been hurt too, and it feels horrible. Please strengthen me so that I can love my enemy, do good to them, and bless them. Please help me desire to pray for them. Amen.

Being the first to say sorry

> **"Don't sin by letting anger control you." Don't let the sun go down while you are still angry, for anger gives a foothold to the devil.**
>
> EPHESIANS 4:26-27

Most kids love climbing anything they can—trees, walls, fences. How about you? Have you ever climbed really high? Maybe on one of those climbing walls that you try to scale while harnessed to a safety rope?

Regardless of what you're climbing, the initial step is the same: *You need to find your first foothold.* Once you've found that, it's much easier to make progress.

In today's reading, Paul is saying that the devil, too, needs a foothold in order to make progress. Anger is an example. If we let it, anger starts to control us, making us do things we'll regret, which will lead to more trouble. That's exactly the kind of destruction the devil wants to make progress in!

When we've had a fight with someone, it's tempting to wallow in the anger that we feel. So, how do we get rid of it? First, think about this: Regardless of who started the argument, it's likely that some of the unkind words were said by us. So, we can counter our anger by saying sorry as soon as possible.

Paul recommends we do this by the end of the day. That may not always be possible, but it is a good reminder not to let arguments drag on for days and weeks.

Once we've taken that brave step to be the first to say "sorry," we may find that the other person finds it a lot easier to apologize too.

CONVERSATION STARTERS

- What do you find hard about saying sorry?
- Imagine the devil on a climbing wall (I know, it's weird, but stay with me . . .). What are the kinds of "footholds" he's climbing on? How can you stop him from making progress?
- It's not always easy to see things from someone else's perspective. Take a look at Philippians 2:3–4 for an attitude check.
- Read Matthew 5:23–24. What is Jesus saying about the importance of reconciling with other people?
- Is there someone you need to say sorry to? It's hard! Talk about it, then ask God for help.

PRAYER

Heavenly God, sometimes it's hard to get along with other people, especially when I think I'm right and they're wrong. But I know you made them too and that you love them. Please help me be the first to make peace when I argue with someone. Amen.

Getting along with others (even when they're annoying!)

Make allowance for each other's faults, and forgive anyone who offends you. Remember, the Lord forgave you, so you must forgive others.

COLOSSIANS 3:13

A classmate who doesn't play fair at sports.

A squad member who makes fun of you.

A friend who copies your work.

It is seriously hard to get along with others sometimes—whether at school, home, church, or extracurriculars. Why are people so difficult? Why do they say mean stuff? Why can't they just be . . . perfect?

Before we answer that question, let's ask another: Are we holding others to higher standards than we hold for ourselves? Is there anything about our own words, thoughts, and actions that can be unkind too?

Making "allowance for each other's faults" helps us get along with those who are difficult. It reminds us that we all have faults. Just as others make allowance for our faults, we can make allowance for theirs.

And wait, Paul is not just encouraging us to make allowance for others. He's also urging us to forgive them.

To be clear, forgiveness doesn't let someone off the hook. In addition to forgiving someone, we may also need to tell a teacher or coach what happened or set boundaries with a person who has mistreated us. But when we forgive someone, we're letting go of the way their actions or words made us feel.

Finally, Paul reminds us of why we're able to forgive. It's because Jesus has forgiven us! All the wrong things we've ever done or will do have been forgiven. When we realize the awesomeness of this, it becomes easier to forgive others, too.

CONVERSATION STARTERS

- Who are you struggling to get along with right now? How do you think Jesus would act if he had to live alongside this person?
- If Jesus was a member of a sports team, how would he deal with difficult team members?
- What is the hardest thing about getting along with those you don't want to work with? Can you think of a loving way to deal with this issue? If you need help, which fruit of the Spirit (Galatians 5:22–23) could you ask God for help with this?
- How do you think Jesus was able to forgive those who crucified him (Luke 23:34)?
- Read Matthew 18:21–35. What does this parable teach us about forgiveness?

PRAYER

Lord Jesus, I don't always find it easy to get along with others—but I know I'm not always easy to work with either. Please help me to work well with other people, and give me a heart of forgiveness toward those who hurt me. In your name, amen.

Setting boundaries

Although Jesus loved Martha, Mary, and Lazarus, he stayed where he was for the next two days.

JOHN 11:5-6

Jesus's good friend Lazarus is sick—really sick. His sisters, Mary and Martha, send Jesus a message, fully expecting that he will come straight away. But he doesn't. Why?

(Ready for some spoilers? You've been warned . . .)

Well, Jesus knows that God is going to do something pretty epic: he's going to raise Lazarus from death. But for that to happen, obviously Lazarus has to die first. If Jesus goes right when he's called, he will heal Lazarus—but that's not God's plan here.

It's a pretty jaw-dropping story. But what can it teach us?

Jesus is showing us a great example of setting boundaries. Boundaries are decisions we make that protect us, and those around us, from unhealthy patterns of behavior. In this case, Mary and Martha want Jesus to come right away. Instead of doing what *they* expect, Jesus puts the situation in God's hands, doing what *he* expects instead.

How does this look in your life? Perhaps it's a friend who expects you to reply immediately to their messages, or sulks when they don't get their way, or insists on coming to your house when it's not convenient.

It is OK to set boundaries by gently telling others how they can and can't treat us, because we're living to please God before we please those around us. And when we set boundaries, guess what? It helps the other person, too, as they learn how to consider others first.

CONVERSATION STARTERS

- Have you heard the term "people-pleaser"? What does it mean? Do you think this term ever applies to you?
- What if we decided to be a "God-pleaser" instead? How would you find out what pleases God? Romans 12:2 might give you a clue!
- Is there someone in your life right now who needs a boundary around how they're treating you? Discuss with your parent or a grown-up what kinds of words you might use to communicate this.
- Read the whole story about Lazarus in John 11:1–44. What do you find amazing about it? What questions do you have?
- Jesus set boundaries throughout his life. Take a look at Matthew 14:23, Mark 3:1–6, and John 2:1–4. What kind of boundary is Jesus setting in each example? How is he pleasing God first?

PRAYER

Dear God, following Jesus's example, I want to be someone who pleases you first. Help me to honor you in my friendships by setting boundaries where they are needed. I pray that these boundaries would also turn my friends' eyes toward you, rather than have them look to me for what only you can provide. Amen.

WEEK 6

Everyone else is doing it—but I don't want to

> **But you belong to God, my dear children. You have already won a victory over those people, because the Spirit who lives in you is greater than the spirit who lives in the world.**
>
> 1 JOHN 4:4

Have you ever been in a situation where other people were doing something you didn't feel comfortable with?

Or maybe they were doing something that tempted you or made you feel pressured, so you joined in but regretted it later?

From childhood through adulthood, we are always going to be impacted by those around us. I'm afraid peer pressure continues, even after you leave school! Sometimes others are doing wonderful things that we can join—but other times, what they're doing is not God's best for them or for us.

At times like this, John encourages us that we *belong to God*. We don't *belong* to our friends, classmates, teachers, or even our parents. We have nothing to prove! We are God's. He loves us and calls us to live for him.

John reminds us that "the Spirit who lives in you is greater than the spirit who lives in the world." Even though we might feel a strong pull toward doing something that isn't right or healthy for us, the Holy

Spirit can pull stronger! As we lean into God, asking him to fill us with his Holy Spirit, we'll find it easier to resist the pressure of others.

CONVERSATION STARTERS

- Can you think of something your friends or classmates do or have done that you don't want to get involved with?
- What kinds of pressures do you think Jesus might have had to resist when he was a kid?
- Check out Luke 4:1–13. What was the devil tempting Jesus with on each occasion?
- Look again at Luke 4:1–13. How was Jesus able to resist temptation?
- What kind of words could you use next time you're asked to join in with something you don't feel is right for you? Come up with a set statement or two, and try saying them out loud. (It might feel awkward at first, but remember why you're doing it.)

PRAYER

Dear Lord, please fill me with your Holy Spirit today and every day. Give me strength to resist the temptation to do things that are not your will. Help others to see Jesus through the integrity you give me. In Jesus's name, amen.

Dealing with bullies

> **"Do not rebel against the Lord, and don't be afraid of the people of the land . . . They have no protection, but the Lord is with us! Don't be afraid of them!"**
>
> **NUMBERS 14:9**

There are many reasons people bully others. Often, a bully has experienced bullying themselves. They may not have had much love shown to them, nor had opportunities to develop their interests in a way that gives them positive ways to spend their time.

A bully might be jealous of others or have low self-esteem. Belittling others makes them feel better about themselves.

In today's passage, Joshua is urging the Israelites not to be afraid of bullies. Let's backtrack a little and catch up on the story . . .

God has instructed the Israelites to claim the land of Canaan. Moses sends some men to explore, and they return, reporting that the new land looks incredible—but its residents are really strong. The Israelites are scared. If they want to keep their heads attached to their bodies, maybe it's best to back off.

But Joshua knows that if it's God's plan for them to live here, he will make it happen. It doesn't matter how fearsome its people are; they'll be no match for God.

I suspect you're not planning to conquer a city anytime soon. But be encouraged that any bully in your life has virtually no power compared to the God you worship. You don't need to be afraid of speaking up when you're being bullied. God sees you, he loves you, and he will resolve the situation. So, step with no fear into the life God has given you.

CONVERSATION STARTERS

- Have you been bullied before? Are you being bullied now? How does it feel? (Note: If you are being bullied in any way, please have this conversation with a trusted grown-up who can help.)
- If Jesus were by your side, what do you think he would say to the bullies?
- Have you ever felt like someone being verbally or physically aggressive toward you stopped you from being the person God created you to be? In what way?
- Read the whole story in Numbers 13 and 14. The Israelites faced a serious consequence for their lack of faith in God. What was it?
- Check out these verses: Joshua 1:9; Psalm 62:7; Psalm 121:3. Which one speaks to you the most? Can you memorize it to encourage you in times of bullying?

PRAYER

Father God, I thank you that I am who *you* say I am—not what the bullies think of me. Please help me to stand firm when they try to ruin my day. Please give me strength to step into everything you have in store for me. In your name, amen.

WEEK 8

Defending those who can't defend themselves

> **Speak up for those who cannot speak for themselves; ensure justice for those being crushed.**
>
> PROVERBS 31:8

Do you know someone who can't speak for themself?

You may know someone who is physically unable to speak. But there are other reasons people might not be able to speak up about their situation. They might lack the confidence, education, status, money, or power to do so. They fear no one will listen to them. Or they are fearful of what might happen to them if they speak.

If our lives are fairly comfortable (for example, if we have food to eat and clothes to wear), it can be easy to forget about those who are in harder situations. Why should we be concerned with those living in war zones, political oppression, poverty, or other situations of hardship, abuse, or persecution?

Because as Christians, Jesus calls us to be concerned about other people as if it were *us* who were suffering. We should be bothered by the fact that some people don't have access to clean drinking water, or education, or that there's a kid at school who is regularly treated poorly by others. As we put ourselves in another person's shoes, these things should rile us up.

God wants us to use our voices on behalf of those who can't. When we see that something looks wrong, will we be brave and speak up?

CONVERSATION STARTERS

- What do you think it means to "have someone's back" or "be an upstander"? What kind of things might you say or do?
- Is there anyone you know in your daily life who would appreciate you being this person for them right now? How can you take action?
- Which situation of injustice around the world right now angers you the most, and why?
- Read Genesis 1:27–31 to get a picture of how God intended us to live on earth. What can you do about situations far from you that don't reflect God's heart?
- Look up a favorite charity online. What are they doing to speak up for those who cannot? Are there ways you can get involved?

PRAYER

Lord God, you created this world to be so good, and yet everywhere I look there is injustice: from my classroom to the other side of the world. Please help me spot when something is not right, and show me ways I can help bring about your will in these places. Amen.

When I'm getting FOMO

Let us hold tightly without wavering to the hope we affirm, for God can be trusted to keep his promise.

HEBREWS 10:23

Do you get FOMO (fear of missing out)?

If you said "no," I might ask you if you're really, truly sure about that answer! I think we *all* have times when we feel left out or feel we are missing out on what others are enjoying.

For example, perhaps you saw your friend's pictures of their amazing vacation, or their party, or even just what they bought at the mall today. You might think, *Why does he get to visit such a cool place? Why can she afford all the latest fashions when I have to save for months just for a new shirt?*

The problem with FOMO is that it starts to control our mind so we can't think about anything else. We lose gratitude for what we do have. We spend more money than we can afford just to try and keep up with others. And we start acting in ways that aren't really true to ourselves.

We may never have had a desire to visit Disney or buy the particular clothes in our friend's shopping haul. And yet once we see their photos, we immediately feel like we're missing out! Isn't that weird?

Even thousands of years ago, the writer of Hebrews knew that we are all prone to FOMO. That's why he wanted to encourage us to stay focused on the hope we have in Jesus, which never disappoints. He talks about holding tightly, as if we're on a boat in a storm and need to hold on for dear life.

And he reminds us that God can be trusted. That means we can relax in the fact that God has the absolute best plan for our lives. The only FOMO we should have is a fear of missing out on life with him!

CONVERSATION STARTERS

- Can you think of a time recently when you've experienced FOMO? What was it about? Did it affect your behavior or decisions?
- Why do you think we get FOMO? And what do you think Jesus would say in response?
- What kind of a life do you think God wants for you? Think hard on this! Then check out John 10:10 for Jesus's answer.
- Read the full passage in John 10:1–18. Can you name all the things Jesus promises us in this passage?
- FOMO can be more of an issue when we're not confident that God wants the best for us. Ask him to build this confidence in you.

PRAYER

Dear Jesus, the Bible says you bring life that is "rich and satisfying." I want to trust this, but sometimes I get distracted by things that seem more appealing. Please help me trust you first and enjoy your priceless gifts without FOMO. In your name, amen.

Crushes

Promise me, O women of Jerusalem, by the gazelles and wild deer, not to awaken love until the time is right.

SONG OF SOLOMON 3:5

Have you read Song of Songs?

It is an eight-chapter love poem written by King Solomon (sometimes called "Song of Solomon"). If you read more, take note: it's pretty intense!

It reminds us that God has created romantic love. It's not wrong to have a crush on someone—God designed us to find other people attractive. But even in this steamy part of the Bible, it's interesting that we're told "not to awaken love until the time is right." It's written three times (2:7, 3:5, and 8:4), so it must be important.

Kids develop at different times, and it's normal to have crushes, a boyfriend or girlfriend, or no romantic relationship at all. Your parents or caregivers may have rules, such as not having a boyfriend or girlfriend until a certain age. All that said, it can be confusing knowing what to do with all the deep feelings you have once they arise!

No matter where you (or your parents) stand on the issue, what's most important at this time in your life is finding out who God has made you to be. That way, if or when God does give you a romantic partner, you will already have a secure sense of identity in him. This will help your relationship to be a healthy, life-giving one.

CONVERSATION STARTERS

- Do your friends talk about crushes?
- How do you think Jesus would contribute to these conversations if he were a kid in your friendship group?
- Where have you seen an example of a really positive dating relationship? And have you seen one that didn't go so well? What do you think makes the positive relationship special?
- Read about the fruits of the Spirit in Galatians 5:22–23. If you have time, read the whole section (verses 16–26). Which of these fruits do you see in the adult relationships you know? Maybe a couple at church, in your family, or among friends or neighbors?
- Read the story of Jacob, Leah, and Rachel in Genesis 29:15–30. Which of the fruits of the Spirit did Jacob have to exercise in his love for Rachel?

PRAYER

Dear Lord, thank you for the people around me and for the feelings of caring that they fill me with. Please help me to trust your timing. If and when you bring me a partner, please help us to treat one another with the honor we both deserve as your child. Thank you. Amen.

WEEKS
11-17

HOME

AND

FAMILY

Getting along with siblings (even when they're frustrating!)

Always be humble and gentle. Be patient with each other, making allowance for each other's faults because of your love.

EPHESIANS 4:2

How do you feel about your sibling/s?

I'm writing this in the summer, and we've set up badminton in the garden, which my kids love to play. It's an absolute joy to watch them laughing and having fun together.

But sometimes, the game creates tension: *"They're not letting me play!" "They've had too long!" "It's my turn!" "They won't play doubles with me!"*

Maybe you can relate to the ups and downs of living with siblings? One moment, it's great fun. The next moment, you wish you were an only child! If you *are* an only child, think of a cousin, neighbor, or friend you see often. Can you relate?

God puts us in relationships with others to love one another, and through that love, we can grow our patience. Siblings are the perfect training ground for us to develop patience. We spend a lot of time with them in close quarters. They may have a habit that really grates on us. They have different personalities and character quirks than us, and it can get frustrating if they don't do things the same way we do.

In this passage, Paul talks about being patient with one another, making allowance for their faults. Learning to be patient with our siblings means we will know how to be much more patient when we leave home and have to deal with annoying roommates or frustrating coworkers.

How can we practice patience, though, when our siblings are really annoying us?

By being "humble and gentle," remembering that we, too, have our flaws, and that all of us live under God's authority.

CONVERSATION STARTERS

- Did you know Jesus grew up with siblings? (They're mentioned in Matthew 12:47, Mark 3:31, Luke 8:19, John 7:3, and Acts 1:14.) What kind of a brother do you think he would have been?
- Name a habit of your sibling's or another relative or neighbor that you find really annoying. What would it look like to be "humble and gentle" next time they do this?
- What kind of a brother or sister (or relative or neighbor) are you? How are you considerate of their needs?
- Read Matthew 11:28–30. How does Jesus describe himself? Does this encourage you? If so, how?

PRAYER

Father God, I don't always find it easy to get along with my siblings, but I trust that we're meant to be in each other's lives. Please help me to be humble and gentle, as Jesus was. May we build a strong relationship that lasts our whole lives. Amen.

WEEK 12

Chores are bores

Work willingly at whatever you do, as though you were working for the Lord rather than for people.

COLOSSIANS 3:23

When you're asked to tidy your room, put away clothes, or clean up after dinner, what's your response? Do you do it willingly? Or do you complain that you're being treated unfairly?

It's tempting to whine about chores when an adult asks us to do them. But imagine it is God asking you. Would that change things? Imagine God watching you as you do the chore—would that affect your effort levels? Because—spoiler alert—he is!

God has created us to work in community—and a community works best when everyone contributes. At home, chores are a wonderful way of playing your part in the family God has given you. At school, helping a teacher or buddying up with a new student are ways that God can bless others through your presence.

Think about this: Chores are not just boring things to moan about—they are actually amazing ways for you to feel part of, and bring value to, your communities. You are God's design—not designed to just have fun while others cater to your every need (although that might be nice). We are all designed to serve others in our unique way, with our own unique personality. No one can set the table like you can!

CONVERSATION STARTERS

- What kind of chores are you responsible for at home or elsewhere? What is your attitude toward them?
- Next time you do a chore, imagine God has personally asked you, and remember he is watching. How does this change your attitude toward it?
- What kind of chores do you think Jesus might have been asked to do when he was your age? Can you picture him doing them? What do you think this looked like?
- Read 2 Thessalonians 3:6–13. Why does Paul feel so strongly about the believers working hard and not leading "idle" lives?
- Take a look at Proverbs 12:14. What kind of rewards do you think hard work might bring?

PRAYER

Dear Lord, I don't always like doing chores—they're boring, and I'd rather be doing something fun. But I know they have to be done, and they will be a blessing to others once completed. Please help me to remember that I'm working for you and to do my chores willingly as my part of the effort. Amen.

"But all the other parents said yes!"

> **Fathers, do not provoke your children to anger by the way you treat them. Rather, bring them up with the discipline and instruction that comes from the Lord.**
>
> **EPHESIANS 6:4**

It's hard feeling left out because of decisions our parents or caregivers have made for us. When it feels like everyone else is allowed to do or own something that we're not, we can become resentful.

But parents have a tough job. In this passage, Paul is urging them not to provoke their children but to raise them according to what God says. It's up to your parent to make decisions that allow you to flourish as an individual—that's not always easy. We may not even understand why they make the decisions they do!

Sometimes, the decisions they make might be different from the ones your friends' parents have made for them. Perhaps they want to protect you from harm. Or they may feel strongly for another reason. And they're willing to risk whatever you or others might think of them so you'll be safe and healthy.

If your parents are seeking the Lord's will as they parent you, you can trust that they are trying to make godly decisions on your behalf. But even if they don't follow Jesus, they still want what is best for you. You may feel comfortable respectfully asking why they made that decision, and that's okay. Their life experience just might give them a viewpoint you haven't considered.

Either way, God calls us to honor our parents, understanding that the decisions they make for us are their attempts to be the best parents they can be—even if we disagree!

CONVERSATION STARTERS

- Can you think of a decision your caregivers made that you didn't agree with? How did you respond, and how was the situation resolved?
- Which areas do you commonly disagree with your parents about? Why do you think they hold the views they do? And why do you hold yours?
- Read Exodus 20:12. This is one of the ten commandments. Does that surprise you? Why/why not?
- Read the context of today's passage: Ephesians 6:1–4. How many pieces of advice does Paul give families? What are the reasons he gives? Can you think of more reasons?
- Check out this story from Jesus's childhood in Luke 2:41–52. How did Jesus and his parents differ in their opinions? How did Jesus honor his parents?

PRAYER

Dear Jesus, It's not always easy to honor my parents when they're not letting me do something others are allowed to do. When this happens, please help me to trust that they want what's best for me. Help us to resolve our disagreements with peace. Amen.

Gratitude is more than words—it's something we do

Be thankful in all circumstances, for this is God's will for you who belong to Christ Jesus.

1 THESSALONIANS 5:18

Do you find it easy to be grateful for the people and things around you? Or do you go through life grumbling when things don't go your way?

I think many of us are a bit of both—but that's the problem. When we have a fantastic birthday party or go on a fun vacation, it's easy to feel grateful. But when the homework is piling up, we've been told to tidy our room, and it's our least favorite meal for dinner again—maybe it's a different story.

Surely, Paul can't mean we need to be thankful in *these* circumstances? Or can he?

Well, it's important to know that Paul experienced suffering that most of us will never face. He was frequently beaten and imprisoned for preaching the gospel. Shortly before writing 1 Thessalonians, he was forced out of the city of Thessalonica for preaching.

And yet, Paul is still able to find things to be thankful for. All through his letters, you'll find messages of thanksgiving—for the people he has met, their growing faith, and their generosity and hospitality.

You may find a lot to complain about when it comes to your family and home life. But even outside of religion, scientists have discovered that gratitude actually releases dopamine and serotonin ("feel good" hormones) to our brain while also reducing the stress hormone cortisol.

When the God who designed us—and knows how our brains work—tells us (through Paul) to give thanks, it seems like a good time to sit up and listen. Gratitude is good for us and those around us!

CONVERSATION STARTERS

- Even when life is hard (as it may be now), what kind of things do you have that you can be grateful for? Consider making a list that you can keep and refer to the next time you're having a difficult day.
- If Jesus were living your life today, what kinds of things do you think he would be grateful for?
- Check out Philippians 1:3–5 and Colossians 1:3–5. What is Paul able to give thanks for at the start of these letters?
- Read Philippians 4:10–20. Paul was in prison when he wrote this letter. How do you think he is able to be so positive? What is the "secret" he refers to in verse 12? (Verse 13 will give you a clue!)
- How might gratitude turn difficult family situations into something positive?

PRAYER

Dear Jesus, I am in awe of Paul, who was so full of thanksgiving even when his life was awful. Please lift my spirits when life is hard by helping me find things to be grateful for. Please change the atmosphere of my home and daily life through gratitude. Amen.

Honoring my parents (really?)

> **"Honor your father and mother. Then you will live a long, full life in the land the Lord your God is giving you.**
>
> **EXODUS 20:12**

Does it feel easy to honor your parents?

We often reserve our worst attitudes for those closest to us—partly because we spend so much time together. It's easy to get frustrated with people we have to put up with each day. It's also because we know we are loved unconditionally—for example, angry outbursts or slammed doors won't change our parents' love for us.

God has designed families to be places where children grow and flourish, eventually becoming independent adults themselves. He asks parents to take seriously the job of raising their children—and he asks children to honor their parents. This is because they're using the wisdom they've gained through life to make good decisions for their children.

This passage is part of the ten commandments that God gave to Moses for the Israelites, and they're still important for us today, even though it may seem impossible to live up to this standard. That's why Jesus came: to die for the stuff we do wrong.

We honor our parents by staying within the boundaries they've set for us, apologizing when we do something wrong, showing them kindness, and speaking respectfully of them to others.

And when we don't live up to this? We can turn to Jesus! He forgives us and gives us a fresh start every time. Thanks to him, we can have a beautiful relationship with our Father God as well as our earthly parents—despite our mistakes and theirs. Jesus's blood has paid the price for us.

CONVERSATION STARTERS

- If Jesus switched places with you this week, what kinds of things do you think he would do and not do in order to honor your parents?
- Is it possible to honor parents even when we don't agree with them? How?
- Can you think of an area where you're struggling to honor your parents?
- Why do you think God says, in today's verse, that honoring your parents leads to a "long, full life"?
- Look at Exodus 2:1–10. How did Miriam honor her mother in this situation?

PRAYER

Lord God, you have asked me to honor my parents, which is sometimes easy and sometimes not. Please show me each day how I can honor you by honoring them. And when I get it wrong, thank you for forgiving me. In Jesus's name, amen.

Dealing with family conflict

> **"If another believer sins against you, go privately and point out the offense. If the other person listens and confesses it, you have won that person back."**
>
> MATTHEW 18:15

We all experience family conflict from time to time.

From time to time? Who are we kidding? Disagreements and drama are a daily occurrence in most households!

From a sister who takes your clothes without asking, to a little brother who's *really* loud, to parents who are just *old* and don't understand . . . family conflict is alive and well.

But in fact, God has a lot to teach us through conflict. Throughout life, we will meet people who disagree with us or treat us unfairly. Learning how to resolve conflict *now,* in the safety of families who love us (yup, even that annoying little brother), will give us coping ninja skills for life.

So what does the Bible have to say about how we resolve conflict?

Firstly, we're to "go privately." Screaming our conflict for the whole house to hear, or getting other siblings to take our side, might not be the best way to sort out an issue. When we're in a calm place, we can go quietly to the other person without the whole family hearing.

Secondly, we're to "point out the offense." Now I bet we're all experts at telling our family members what they've done wrong! But this isn't a point-the-finger exercise—it's more about explaining how that person has hurt us. We can do this calmly and gently, without hurting their feelings.

And if this doesn't work? That's when we get others involved—ideally a parent, or perhaps an older sibling who can help without taking sides.

CONVERSATION STARTERS

- When we experience conflict with a family member, one common response is to give them the silent treatment. Based on today's reading, why isn't this the approach Jesus would choose?
- Are you in the middle of any family conflict right now? Who with? Are there actions you need to take?
- How do you think conflict can work to make relationships stronger?
- Read Genesis 27 to discover the story of two brothers in deep conflict. Then read Genesis 33 to learn about their reconciliation. What encourages you from this story?
- Read 2 Peter 3:14. How might you be described as living a peaceful life? Or is this something you're working on? Or need to work on?

PRAYER

Father God, I know you've given me my family to love and be loved by—but sometimes they're so annoying! When we have conflict, please guide me as to how I can respond in a godly, peaceful way. And please strengthen our relationships! Amen.

I am a blessing!

> **The human body has many parts, but the many parts make up one whole body. So it is with the body of Christ.**
>
> 1 CORINTHIANS 12:12

We receive so much from our families: love, safety, security—not to mention food, clothes, money, and education. Sometimes it's easy to forget that we have things we can give them in return.

This is why I've chosen to end this section on Home and Family with a reminder that *you* have an important role to play in your family.

In today's verse, Paul likens the "body of Christ" (or the "family of believers") to a human body. All the parts of your body have an important role to play. Perhaps you've had the experience of breaking an arm or leg, or you have a more permanent disability. You'll know how hard it can be not to have part of your body function as it should.

Similarly, Paul is saying that when we don't play our part in the body of Christ, it becomes super hard for the body to work properly. This is true at church, at school, and at home—every time you connect with others, it's like a little section of the body of Christ.

God has made you unique. Perhaps you can think of people who share your talents and interests—but nobody has them in the exact combination and quantity that you do. You bring something special to the world—and to your family. You're not just there to receive, but to give.

So don't be down on yourself or what you have to contribute—you are important, and you can be a huge blessing!

CONVERSATION STARTERS

- Have you ever been part of a group or team that didn't function well? Why do you think it didn't work?
- What difference do you think Jesus would make to your family if he was part of it? How is Jesus working through you when you spend time with your family?
- Can you think of five ways you can bless your family by contributing your gifts? How about one way you could bless them today?
- Take a look at 1 Corinthians 3:5–9. How did Paul and Apollos both contribute to the task of sharing the gospel? Is one contribution more important than the other?
- Read the full passage in 1 Corinthians 12:12–27. How does this help you understand the role you play in your family?

PRAYER

Dear Jesus, thank you for making me unique and placing me in a family where I can be a blessing. Help me to know what that looks like, and give me the strength to bless others each day, even when I'm not feeling like it. In your name, amen.

WEEKS
18-25

SCHOOL

WEEK 18

When classmates won't pull their weight

> **For God called you to do good, even if it means suffering, just as Christ suffered for you. He is your example, and you must follow in his steps.**
>
> 1 PETER 2:21

If you go to school or are part of a homeschool cooperative, you probably work on projects or presentations with others.

When you're teamed up with someone who's fun and super creative with loads of ideas and a strong work ethic, it's bliss, right?

But when your partner drags their feet and leaves you to do all the work? Not so much.

In this passage, Peter is reminding believers that acting in a godly way—doing what Jesus would do—sometimes feels hard. But that doesn't mean we stop doing the right thing.

Sometimes we have to work—or even live—with people we haven't chosen to work with, or on a project we're not interested in. Life might feel unfair when others don't do as much as they should, and we're stuck working on something we find difficult or boring.

What does Peter say to us? We are called to do good! Not just when others are doing it and it's easy, but even when they're not doing it. We do good because Jesus did good to us and for us, even while he was suffering.

Next time you're feeling the injustice of lazy team members (or siblings!), ask yourself what Jesus would do in that situation. Remember, God has given you a role to play and talents to offer. Do the best you can—not because your teammates deserve your best, but because God does.

CONVERSATION STARTERS

- Have you ever been in a situation where you were doing a greater amount of work than others in the same group? How did it feel?
- Take a look at Luke 10:38–42. How did Martha feel? How did Jesus respond? Are there times when it's right to stop work for something else?
- Read the parable of the prodigal son in Luke 15:11–32. If you know the story already, look at verses 28–32. How does the older son feel? But what has his father already given him?
- Check out Matthew 20:1–16. Why are those who were hired first complaining? How does the landowner respond?
- What do these stories teach us about "doing good" even when others are not?

PRAYER

Dear Jesus, you know how it feels to suffer unfairly. I don't like doing all the work when others are being lazy. But I know you have called me to do good. Help me know when to work, and when to stop. In your name, amen.

I don't understand!

"Don't be afraid, for I am with you. Don't be discouraged, for I am your God. I will strengthen you and help you. I will hold you up with my victorious right hand."

ISAIAH 41:10

How do you feel when you get stuck on a problem?

Maybe it's a complicated math problem or a piece of creative writing that you're out of ideas for. Perhaps it's a geographical diagram that seems to make no sense—or a history essay that feels impossible.

It's a horrible feeling not knowing how to begin to tackle an assignment. But have you ever thought of God as the master mathematician? The greatest author there's ever been? The creator of the earth, the weather, and all of geography? Sovereign over all history? Did you know he's interested in your schoolwork—and can even help you with it?

This verse from Isaiah is spoken to the whole nation of Israel. Isaiah has warned them that if they don't put God first, other nations will invade and capture them. But this verse says that, even when that happens, God will not abandon his people. He will send help—at first, by allowing them to return to their own country, and eternally, by sending Jesus to be their Savior.

There is no situation too big or too small that we cannot bring before God. He is there when our country is being invaded, and he's there when we can't figure out the math equation. He never abandons us, and he longs to help us. All we need to do is ask.

CONVERSATION STARTERS

- What are some ways God might help you with your work?
- Is there a subject or topic you find difficult? Why not ask God for help now? Be specific—God understands it all!
- No one is good at everything—and this doesn't change, even as you leave school and go into the workplace. How do you think your education is preparing you for adult life?
- Check out Exodus 4:10–17. God called Moses to ask Pharaoh to free the Israelites from slavery, but Moses didn't feel confident at public speaking. God helped Moses in two ways (v.12 and v.16)—what were they?
- Take a look at Matthew 14:24–32. What did Jesus help Peter to do? What made Peter struggle? What can we learn from this?

PRAYER

Father God, thank you for being with me, helping me and giving me strength. Please help me understand ___________ (subject/topic you're finding difficult). I'm finding it really hard right now. I would love to get better at it and understand your world more. Thank you. Amen.

A build-up of pressure

> **"So don't worry about tomorrow, for tomorrow will bring its own worries. Today's trouble is enough for today."**
>
> MATTHEW 6:34

Do you sometimes feel pressured to achieve well academically?

Whether it comes from your teachers, parents, or within yourself, pressure can turn into stress that feels impossible to shift.

A little bit of stress can be good for us, helping us work hard on what's in front of us. But too much stress makes it harder for us to focus and succeed.

Often the pressure comes because we (or those around us) are looking to the future. We want to get a good job, which means getting a good degree, which means getting good grades *now*.

Looking to the future is not a bad thing in itself—but Jesus reminds us, in this part of Matthew (called the Sermon on the Mount), that we can't predict the future. An estimated 65 percent of children beginning elementary school this year will end up in jobs that don't even exist yet! Think about it—the world is always changing. Part of my current job—blogging and digital marketing—didn't exist when I was at school.

Jesus reminds us that there will be other things to worry about "tomorrow" (which could mean the day after today, next week, next year, or next decade!). Instead, we can focus our eyes and hearts on the challenges before us *today*.

Yes, work hard. Yes, do your best. But anytime you feel that pressure rising, remember this: You can only do what you're capable of doing today. Do it well, glorify God, and you will grow into the person he made you to be, capable of dealing with tomorrow's worries when they come—and not a moment before.

CONVERSATION STARTERS

- Can you remember a time you became stressed about school work or exam results?
- How do you deal with pressure? Do you have ways of reducing it so it doesn't become unmanageable?
- What's something in the future that you feel stressed about? How can you use Jesus's presence and this lesson to think about it in a different way?
- How did Jesus deal with pressure so it didn't mount up? (Luke 5:15–16 may give you a clue.)
- Read Luke 22:41–44, which happened just before Jesus was arrested. We now know sweating blood to be a condition called hematidrosis, an extremely rare reaction in cases of extreme stress. How did Jesus respond to this stress?

PRAYER

Dear Jesus, you know what it's like to feel under pressure, and I'm grateful that you're with me when I'm feeling like this. Give me strength to deal with each day as it comes. Help me not to worry about the future, trusting that you know what's coming. Amen.

I am unique

For we are God's masterpiece. He has created us anew in Christ Jesus, so we can do the good things he planned for us long ago.

EPHESIANS 2:10

When I was 10, my small elementary school picked the girls' netball team. Netball requires a team of seven players, and there were nine girls in our class. You guessed it—I was one of the two not chosen.

I'm fortunate that my school chose the team in a very kind way, which didn't make me feel bad—but still, I was aware that I was not as gifted in sports as others in my class.

School or home education can be a wonderful opportunity to explore all kinds of interests: sports, music, science, art, and so on. Perhaps you get interesting visitors or go on fun field trips.

But education also highlights areas where we struggle. When others around us are much better at things than we are, it can cause us to wonder, *What am I good at?*

Paul knew that all sorts of people—not just preteens—feel down about themselves or their abilities. So he emphasized that we are God's masterpiece. It isn't our own skills that make us awesome; it's the fact that God created us!

And that's not all: Paul goes on to say that God has created "good things" for each of us to do, which we're able to do because Jesus enables us.

So next time you're feeling frustrated about your abilities, remember, you are unique! God has designed you with unique talents and ways to use those unique talents for good.

CONVERSATION STARTERS

- What do you imagine Jesus might have been really good at when he was your age?
- Which subject area most frequently gets you down because it feels too hard to understand?
- Which subject, interest, or hobby makes you light up because you love it so much?
- Read 1 Samuel 16:1–13 about Samuel anointing the next king. Who did he think it would be? And who had God actually chosen?
- Re-read verse 7. What do you think it means that "God looks at the heart"? What is God's priority for each one of us?

PRAYER

Lord God, sometimes I wish I were better at __________ (insert something you find hard), but I know you have created me uniquely. Please help me discover the things you've designed me to be skilled at, and give me opportunities to do good. Amen.

Getting along with teachers (even when we don't click)

Everyone must submit to governing authorities. For all authority comes from God, and those in positions of authority have been placed there by God.

ROMANS 13:1

How do you feel about your teachers?

Maybe your current teacher is brilliant—or perhaps you wish you still had last year's teacher.

It can be hard to work for a teacher we don't like. We might feel that they don't like us, they have class favorites, or their sense of humor falls flat.

However we feel about our teachers, God has placed them in authority over us. They have the necessary teaching qualifications—and, through an interviewing process, your school has decided they are the right person to employ. Even if we don't find them easy or likable, they've earned the right to be in the classroom, doing their job.

So how do we get along with them when it's hard? Paul says we are to submit to them—in other words, do what they say. Even when we're not happy with our teacher, we can realize that our job is to do the work they've assigned. We don't have to *love* every teacher; we just need to recognize their role in our lives as someone there to teach.

(PS: Very occasionally, a teacher is found to not be doing the job they should be doing. If you think a teacher is behaving inappropriately, please inform your caregivers, who can contact the school or give you guidance on what to do.)

CONVERSATION STARTERS

- Out of all the teachers you've had, who were the easiest/hardest to get along with?
- If Jesus was a kid in your class, how do you think he would relate to your teacher? What kinds of things would he do/say (or not do/say)?
- Take a look at Romans 13:1–7. What are the reasons Paul gives for honoring those in authority?
- If you currently have a teacher who is hard to get along with, how might you put into practice Paul's words in this passage?
- Read Daniel 1. Daniel was employed by King Nebuchadnezzar, a non-religious king who did not always make good decisions. Who did Daniel obey first—God or the king? How did it turn out for him? What does this teach us?

PRAYER

Dear God, I know I can trust you when I ask you to be king of my life. But I don't always find it easy to honor the teachers you've given me. Please help me to be kind and respectful and to do the right thing. Amen.

Preparing for a test

We ask God to give you complete knowledge of his will and to give you spiritual wisdom and understanding. Then the way you live will always honor and please the Lord.

COLOSSIANS 1:9B-10A

Full disclosure: Today's verse is not specifically about preparing for a test. Paul was not attempting to encourage the Colossians while they studied the water cycle for a geography exam!

But Paul *is* reminding the Colossians that God knows everything, and that his ways are perfect.

When we're preparing for a test, God can help us in practical ways. He knows everything there is to know about clouds and planets, because he made them. He understands the most complex mathematical problems and scientific equations, because he set them in motion for humans to discover. He understands music and art and literature, because he's the master-creator who poured his creative spirit into the great composers, artists, and writers we learn about today.

There is nothing God doesn't know, and he wants to help us as we prepare to be tested on this stuff!

But God doesn't just want to give us *academic* understanding. He wants to give us *spiritual understanding*. Even more important than our test results (which may feel pretty important right now) is how we live as children of God and citizens of his world.

Test results may get us into a good college and job, but that's it. They are powerless to help us live truly fulfilled lives. Only God can give us the spiritual wisdom we need, helping us to live lives that honor him and those around us. This brings more joy than any academic success!

CONVERSATION STARTERS

- What kinds of tests or challenges do you think Jesus might have faced as a preteen?
- Do you have any tests coming up? How are you feeling about them? Have you told God?
- How does it make you feel that God has all the knowledge you need for your test?
- Read Philippians 1:9–11. What is Paul saying that "really matters"? Is there anything you'd add to the list?
- Read today's verses in context—Colossians 1:9–14. How does God help us with the challenges of life (like tests)? What does he give us?

PRAYER

Dear Lord, I have a test coming up and I'm feeling __________ (tell God how you're feeling). Please focus my mind in the time I have to learn and study. And please help me to grow closer to you, which is more important than getting excellent test results. Amen.

School is a privilege . . . yes, really

> **Whatever is good and perfect is a gift coming down to us from God our Father, who created all the lights in the heavens. He never changes or casts a shifting shadow.**
>
> JAMES 1:17

I'm sure you don't regularly think of school as a "good and perfect gift." (If you do, you are lucky!)

But when we stop to remember all the places in the world where children are not educated—perhaps because of poverty, gender, or lack of resources—we can count ourselves pretty fortunate that we have these kinds of opportunities.

Give some thought to your last school day. How many students were in your class? What age were they? What resources did you use throughout the day? If you are homeschooled, consider the opportunities you have had recently. Where have you been? Who have you learned alongside? What resources did you use?

Now imagine being taught in a hot, buggy classroom with 50 students, all different ages and stages, without enough basic resources (like books or pens, and definitely no laptops) to go around.

James tells us that every "good and perfect" gift comes from God. While not always perfect, education ensures that everyone in society develops the gifts God has given them. This definitely puts it into the category of "good"!

Education is a good gift that God has given us. He could have created us to know everything from birth, but instead he has provided a brilliantly interesting and complex world that we learn about gradually through life—and then we teach others about it!

CONVERSATION STARTERS

- What kind of education do you think Jesus had, and from whom?
- What do you feel grateful for about your education?
- How might a grateful attitude help you when school feels challenging?
- How do your words and actions in school reflect your attitude toward your education?
- Read Psalm 100 (it's only five verses!). What are the reasons offered here for giving thanks to God?

PRAYER

Father God, I don't always love school, but I know it is a privilege to be educated. Thank you for giving me this blessing. Please help me to make the most of my opportunities and to use my education for your glory. In your name, amen.

WEEK 25

What about the future?

> **Trust in the Lord with all your heart; do not depend on your own understanding. Seek his will in all you do, and he will show you which path to take.**
>
> PROVERBS 3:5-6

What do you want to be or do when you're an adult? Have you given it much thought? Has your ideal career changed in the last few years?

It can be fun thinking about the future: all that freedom, an enjoyable job, maybe marriage and children. But grown-up life also comes with challenges: bills to pay, dream jobs we don't get, or relationships that don't work out.

As we get older and adult life draws nearer, our schools will focus more and more on the future. We might start to feel anxious. Will we get the grades for a good college? Will we get that internship? Will we have the finances for a home of our own, or even a car?

God does not promise that life will be easy, but he does promise that if we take each decision to him, he will show us "which path to take."

I'd love to say this is always clear, but the reality is that it's not. In many cases, life is a series of intersections that we arrive at with God and have to spend a little time figuring out whether to turn left or right.

But God can and does guide us—through prayer, his word, our emotions, opportunities, and the wisdom of others.

Anytime we feel worried about the future, we can take that to God, trusting that as we seek him in all we do, he will not let us go astray.

CONVERSATION STARTERS

- As a child, what do you think Jesus knew about his future? What do you think he didn't know?
- Which aspects of your future excite or worry you? If you wish, write a list.
- Why do you think the writer of Proverbs tells us to trust in the Lord and not to "depend on your own understanding"? What is the problem with our understanding compared with the Lord's?
- Read Luke 12:16–21. Jesus told this story about a man who thought his future was safer than it was to demonstrate why trusting in God is so important. What can we learn from it?
- Take a look at Proverbs 4:23–27. What advice does the writer give us for a God-honoring future?

PRAYER

Dear Lord, when I'm worried about the future, remind me to take my emotions to you. Please fill me with your peace about my future. You have promised to never leave me, and I am so grateful. Help me to get better at asking you for guidance and listening for what you say. Amen.

WEEKS 26-34

MENTAL AND EMOTIONAL HEALTH

Speaking about feelings

> **How long must I struggle with anguish in my soul, with sorrow in my heart every day? How long will my enemy have the upper hand?**
>
> **PSALM 13:2**

It's not always easy talking about our feelings. Even if you're usually a chatty person, letting others know when you're struggling can feel vulnerable. But it's much better to talk about feelings than keep them bottled up until they spill out in an unhealthy burst of anger.

David models this really well in the Psalms. Many of them are raw, unfiltered poems of deep distress. David knew that God is big enough to take all our emotions, so he didn't hold back from ranting about everything he was feeling.

We can do the same. We can be 100 percent honest with God. We can write in a journal or speak out loud or in our heads. We can get super-detailed about who or what is bringing us down. We can even blame him. (God is never guilty, because he never sins—but he can take our anger at him anyway!)

God knows what we're thinking, so our words don't shock him. You might wonder why we should say them at all if he already knows. Because communication—even negative communication—grows a relationship. As we yell at God, we actually draw closer to him. We can be honest with those who make us feel loved and safe, and God is the ultimate loving, safe space.

It's wise to have one or two people who we can talk to about our feelings. But if that's not possible right now, know that you can always go to God. He's always listening, and his love for you will never fade, no matter what you say.

CONVERSATION STARTERS

- Can you think of a time when Jesus talked openly to God about his feelings? (If you're not sure, check out Matthew 26:39.) What might it look like for you to talk openly to God? (If you already do this, ask "What does it look like when you talk openly to God?")
- Take a look at Psalm 18:1–3. List all the words and phrases that describe who God is. How might your list help you understand you can trust him?
- Read the whole of Psalm 13. How does it end, and why do you think David can say what he says?
- For more psalms along the same lines as Psalm 13, try Psalms 22, 42, 60, or 102. Which emotions are being expressed in each one? How does the psalmist fix his eyes on God?

PRAYER

Father God, thank you for always being there to listen to me, whatever I am feeling. Please help me to turn to you with my emotions, and please help me to work through them so that I can be all you've created me to be. Thank you. Amen.

Dealing with anxiety

> **Don't worry about anything; instead, pray about everything. Tell God what you need, and thank him for all he has done.**
>
> PHILIPPIANS 4:6

What kinds of things make you worry and feel anxious? Tests? Sleepovers? Leaving the house? New experiences? You are not alone! Many people feel anxious on a regular basis.

God understands anxiety deeply because he created it. If your life has been impacted by anxiety—yours or someone else's—you may wonder why God created something that has the potential to be so damaging.

But God never created anxiety to be an obstacle in our lives. Anxiety helps us to be cautious in situations that could be dangerous. It keeps us safe when we're climbing trees or crossing the road.

Sadly, in the hands of Satan, anxiety can become something that takes over our lives. Satan tells us lies about whether something is safe or not. He causes us to doubt things that are trustworthy or worry about things that haven't happened yet (and probably won't).

So in this passage, Paul is reminding us to take everything we feel anxious about to God. Tell him what you need—whether that's courage for a new situation, peace as you go to the mall, or a clear head as you take that test.

We can also ask God to get rid of the lies that are clouding our minds: lies like, *everything will go wrong, no one will talk to us, we're better off not going*—or whatever other lies we might be fighting. Recognize what Satan might be telling you about a situation, and take it to God to discover what's really true.

CONVERSATION STARTERS

- What kinds of situations cause you anxiety?
- Which of your recent anxieties were genuine worries (*likely* to, or that *did*, happen)? Which ones were lies (*unlikely* to happen)?
- What difference might it make to take all these worries to God?
- Check out Luke 10:38–42. What was Martha anxious about? What was Jesus's response? Ask Jesus now what he wants to say to you in your anxiety, and listen for his response.
- Read Matthew 14:22–31. It was when Peter's anxiety overtook his faith that he began to sink (v.30). This passage comes just after Jesus fed over 5,000 people with five loaves and two fish—an amazing miracle, yet Peter has temporarily forgotten Jesus's power. What has Jesus done in your life that you can remember in times of anxiety?

PRAYER

Dear Jesus, your power helped Peter walk on water, and I know it can help me when I feel anxious, too. Help me to work out what's true and real, and what's a lie. Give me your peace when I don't feel it. And thank you for all you've given me. Amen.

WEEK 28

A feeling of overwhelm

> **Then you will experience God's peace, which exceeds anything we can understand. His peace will guard your hearts and minds as you live in Christ Jesus.**
>
> PHILIPPIANS 4:7

Feeling overwhelmed is a common human experience.

You might feel overwhelmed when you have a busy schedule, a pile of homework, or lots of chores. You might feel it in social situations or when there are a lot of sensory stimuli around you. We don't all get overwhelmed by the same things, but the feeling of overwhelm is one that pretty much all of us get from time to time.

In this part of Philippians, Paul is writing to our minds. He has encouraged us to ask God for what we need (see Week 27: Dealing with anxiety), and now he is reassuring us that God's peace is powerful enough to "guard [our] hearts and minds." What does this mean?

It means that when we go to God first with our anxiety, our overwhelm, our Big Feelings, he can give us a peace that is much, much greater than any sense of peace we get from anything else. It doesn't necessarily mean that our lives will get easier, but it does mean that our hearts and minds will be protected.

Paul also suggests that this overriding sense of peace comes as a result of living "in Christ Jesus"—the two go hand in hand. When we commit our lives to Jesus each day (chatting to him about what's happening and how we're feeling), he will hold us in this peace that "exceeds anything we can understand."

Our lives may be busy and stressful, but we can still know God's peace.

CONVERSATION STARTERS

- Are you feeling overwhelmed right now? What's causing this feeling? Can you describe what overwhelm feels like for you?
- If you're not feeling overwhelmed today, can you think of a recent time when you did? How did it feel?
- Can you think of any situations in Jesus's life where he brought peace to a situation? (Give some thought to it, but look up Matthew 8:23–27, Mark 5:24–34, or John 11:17–27 if you're stuck!)
- Sometimes we are overwhelmed with a task we have to do. Check out the stories of Moses (Exodus 4:1–17), Barak (Judges 4), or Esther (Esther 4). What was the task that threatened to overwhelm them? How did God give them his peace?
- If you're feeling overwhelmed, you might appreciate Psalm 61. Read it slowly. You may like to use it as a prayer whenever you're feeling like this.

PRAYER

Lord God, when I am feeling overwhelmed, please give me your peace. Thank you that it is powerful enough to guard my heart and mind from the situations that threaten to take over. I pray that I would know your peace right now. Amen.

When mood swings are getting me down (and up)

Jesus Christ is the same yesterday, today, and forever.

HEBREWS 13:8

If you've ever felt joyfully elated one moment and close to tears the next, you'll know what a mood swing is.

Mood swings happen throughout life, but certain things make them more frequent, including puberty. As your body and mind start to change, you may find your mood swinging from one extreme to the other. It can be super challenging to manage.

The good news is that *Jesus never changes*. Today's verse reminds us that who Jesus was yesterday is who Jesus is today—and tomorrow he'll be exactly the same. Jesus is the one person we can totally depend on, whose mood does not change by the day.

Who was Jesus "yesterday"? That word means *every time in the past*. So we can look at who Jesus was in the Bible, and we can also remind ourselves of who Jesus has been to us in our life.

In the Bible, we see that Jesus was kind and loving, and that he had no time for those who looked religious on the outside but didn't really love God on the inside. We observe that he served the poor, noticed those who weren't noticed by anyone else, and loved those who no one else loved.

This is the Jesus we're getting to know. He is exactly the same now as he was in the Bible. He can take all your emotions, and will never abandon you or stop loving you. He is 100 percent trustworthy and steadfast.

CONVERSATION STARTERS

- Can you remember a time recently when your mood changed rapidly? What were the factors that affected your mood/s? What helped? What didn't?
- How might imagining Jesus sitting next to you while you're feeling an extreme emotion help you in those moments?
- Read 1 Kings 19:1–9. How did Elijah feel (v.3–4)? What was the reason for this (v.1–2)? How did God help him (v.5–9)?
- Look up Lamentations 3:22. How might this verse encourage you when your mood is all over the place?
- Check out John 20:11–18. How was Mary feeling and why? How did Jesus's presence help her?

PRAYER

Dear Jesus, thank you that you're always with me and always ready to listen to how I'm feeling. Thank you too for loving me unconditionally—not only when I'm happy and easy to be around, but also when I'm feeling low, miserable, disappointed, or furious. Amen.

It's been a bad day

Day and night I have only tears for food, while my enemies continually taunt me, saying, "Where is this God of yours?"

PSALM 42:3

Some people might suggest that those who trust in God should always feel happy. The psalmist who wrote today's verse writes as if people have told him this too. Those around him are questioning God's existence because they believe God should make us happy all the time.

But this isn't a biblical view of life. God has created us to feel lots of different emotions, and they all have a part to play. Remember the *Inside Out* movies? They demonstrate this really well!

No emotions are bad, but when one emotion takes over our mind, it can be hard to function as we were designed to. When this happens, what's the solution? Should we ignore it?

No! It's important to identify our feelings. This isn't just 21st-century psychology—the psalmists knew this to be true too, and they were writing thousands of years ago.

The psalmist who wrote today's verse is honest about his sadness. He's not ignoring it or pushing it to the back of his mind. He's taking time to voice it in poetry. If you've ever tried to write a poem, you know how long that can take! In other words, he's not in a rush to become happy again.

What happens when we tell Jesus about our bad day?

First, we're acknowledging, and not ignoring, our emotions. Second, we're reminding ourselves that it's OK not to feel happy all the time. And third, Jesus responds by meeting us in our feelings and helping us get to a point of peace again—maybe not immediately, but at the right time.

CONVERSATION STARTERS

- If you've had a bad day, why not take it to Jesus now? Voice your feelings to him as precisely as you can (disappointed, frustrated, angry, lonely, exhausted, etc.).
- Think about what you know of Jesus's life. What sorts of things might have contributed to him having bad days?
- What do you think are some advantages of being honest with God about our emotions, rather than bottling them up?
- Check out 1 Peter 5:7. God cares for you! How does this encourage you to be honest with him? Could you memorize this verse to remember on days that don't go well?
- Consider writing a poem about how you feel today. You don't need to show it to anyone, so don't worry about making it publication-worthy! It can just be between you and God.

PRAYER

Dear Jesus, I know you know how it feels to have a bad day. I'm grateful that I can be honest with you about my feelings, and that you always listen, always care, and always help me find peace and joy again. Amen.

A healthy sleep routine

> **It is useless for you to work so hard from early morning until late at night, anxiously working for food to eat; for God gives rest to his loved ones.**
>
> PSALM 127:2

How do you sleep?

Does it take you a long time to fall asleep, or are you out the moment your head hits the pillow? Do you sleep through to morning, or wake up periodically through the night? Are you an early bird, or do you appreciate sleeping late?

Good sleep is an essential ingredient to good mental health. But have you ever considered it a gift from God?

I mean—it makes sense, doesn't it? God created our bodies and our minds, so he knows best what they need to function well. And sleep is a part of that—a gift to us to help us thrive.

Today's Psalm is by Solomon. Our translation uses the word "rest," but many others use the word "sleep." Either way, the meaning is the same: We need to stop work regularly to rest. We will wear ourselves out if we never stop. This applies to hobbies, too. We simply cannot keep launching from one activity to the next without any downtime. Our body and mind will suffer.

Going to sleep is also an act of trust. It's trusting that God will help us on the math test, even though we've stopped studying to go to sleep; that God will be with us in the gymnastics competition, even though we've stopped training. Prioritizing good sleep is a way of saying to God, "I've done what I can; now please step in and do the rest."

CONVERSATION STARTERS

- Think about your sleep pattern. Are you getting enough sleep? What works well? What doesn't work so well? Are there any changes you could make to improve your sleep if it's not as healthy as it could be?
- Can you think of a time when Jesus was asleep? (If not, look up Matthew 8:23–27!) What was happening around him while he slept? Why were the disciples annoyed? Why was Jesus frustrated with them?
- If Jesus can sleep through a storm, what does that tell us about his trust in God?
- How might going to sleep be an act of trust for you?
- Look up Psalm 4:8. Do you believe this? Or is it a struggle to believe this right now? Maybe this could be a verse that you memorize or write out and post above your bed.

PRAYER

Lord God, you are the creator of sleep and the giver of good gifts. Thank you for giving me the gift of sleep, even when I don't find it easy to do. Please grow my trust in you so I can feel your peace about things I've not managed to do or finish by the time I need to sleep. Amen.

I'm sad and I don't know why

> **O Lord, you have examined my heart and know everything about me.**
>
> PSALM 139:1

One of the hardest times to manage our mental health is when there is no logical reason for how we feel.

Our emotions will often go up and down depending on what's happening around us—for example, how people treat us, the grades we get, or even the weather. But sometimes we will feel sad without really knowing why.

This can make us feel a bit adrift—like we're floating around in life with no firm anchor. If we can't pin our sadness (or any other negative emotion) on a reason, we can start to become anxious and fearful, wondering what's wrong with us. We might even feel out of control. If we don't know why we're upset, it becomes harder to think of things that might cheer us up.

The good news is that there is nothing wrong with you if you can't pinpoint the source of your emotions. This happens—you are human! The even better news is that there is One who knows us even better than we know ourselves. In today's Psalm, David states that God knows *everything* about us. He knows what we are feeling and where it comes from. He even knows what we'll feel tomorrow.

We can trust God with our emotions and our triggers, even if we can't understand them ourselves. And we can ask him to be our anchor while we're feeling uncertain or worried.

CONVERSATION STARTERS

- Have you had an experience of feeling a negative emotion with no clear reason or understanding as to why? How did it feel to not know why you were feeling that way?
- What do you think Jesus might say to you in those moments?
- How might Jesus want you to act around friends who are experiencing this?
- What makes it difficult to be close to God when you're not feeling good?
- Check out Psalm 23, especially verse 4. God wants to be close to you and comfort you when you're in "the darkest valley." How does this make you feel?

PRAYER

Dear God, I don't know why I'm feeling this way, but I feel __________ (fill in your emotion). I know that you know what's going on inside my mind, though. Please draw close to me and comfort me, bringing me peace now and hope for the future. Amen.

When I'm feeling angry

People with understanding control their anger;
a hot temper shows great foolishness.

PROVERBS 14:29

When was the last time you got really angry?

All sorts of things can cause this feeling to rise up in us: the actions of our siblings or parents, the decision of a coach, the unfair words of a classmate.

Like with other emotions, it doesn't do any good to ignore our anger or pretend it doesn't exist. But it can also be devastating to act on our anger—this is what's meant by a "hot temper." When we are in a rage, we tend to make poor decisions. We might make a situation worse by what we say or do.

So how do we get this balance right? How can we recognize our anger but not allow it to lead us into an even worse situation?

By learning to control our anger, says the writer of Proverbs. This might be hard in the moment, so the first step is to pause and take a moment to breathe. Next, we can ask God to help us calm down, get some perspective, and see a situation through others' eyes.

We can also let out our anger to God. We can tell him why we're angry and be as furious as we like—he can take it, and it won't make matters worse.

And finally, God might give us someone else we can speak to about it as well—a parent, sibling, or trusted friend. This person will hold our anger with us and help us process it. When we're calm, it'll be easier to sort out the situation, if it's even something we have the power to change.

CONVERSATION STARTERS

- When did you last feel really angry? What was it about, and who/what was your anger directed to?
- Where do you think Jesus is when you feel angry? What's he saying? How is he encouraging or challenging you?
- Read the story of David, Abigail, and Nabal in 1 Samuel 25:1–13. Why has David become angry? And what is his response?
- Now read 1 Samuel 25:14–22. What is Abigail's response to David's anger?
- Finally, read 1 Samuel 25:23–25. What did Abigail ask of David? Why? (Verse 31 might give you a clue.) How did it make a difference?

PRAYER

Lord God, I know that when I get angry, I can start to sin in other ways. Next time I'm angry, please remind me to cool off with you and with those you have put in my life to help me regulate my emotions. Please, calm me down and give me the skills to resolve or accept the situation. Amen.

Jesus can take away my shame

And [Jesus] said to her, "Daughter, your faith has made you well. Go in peace. Your suffering is over."

MARK 5:34

Guilt and shame are two yucky emotions. Can you remember feeling one or both of them recently? Guilt is the feeling you get when you *do* something wrong. Shame is the feeling of *being* wrong (even when you're not).

Why do we feel shame? Sometimes it's because of the bad things we've done. Other times, it's because of bad things people have done to us. We've done nothing wrong, but their actions have brought us shame.

In today's verse, Jesus has just healed a woman who has been bleeding for 12 years. *Twelve years*. Can you imagine? There weren't any pills or operations available to stop the bleeding. And in that culture, bleeding made you unclean. The woman wouldn't have been allowed to socialize with others or even work. She must have felt incredibly isolated.

Was it her fault? Of course not! Yet she carried a huge weight of shame because of her condition. She didn't want to bother Jesus or draw attention to herself—but she did want to get well, and she knew Jesus could help her. So she touched his robe. He could have gone on with his day, but he wanted to bring the woman out of her shame, so he spoke words of compassion and love to her.

If shame is something you feel, know that Jesus can and wants to take that away. He wants to crown you with honor and beauty as the much-loved child of the King that you are!

CONVERSATION STARTERS

- Is shame a feeling you can relate to? Can you pinpoint where it comes from?
- What do you think Jesus would say to you if you touched his robe in a crowd like the woman did?
- Read the full story in Mark 5:25–34. How do you think the woman felt after her encounter with Jesus?
- Check out Psalm 8:3–5. How does it make you feel that the God of all the universe loves and cares for you? Do you find this easy to believe?
- When others speak lies over us, we can turn to the Bible for truth. Try 1 Peter 2:9, Colossians 1:13–14, and Jeremiah 31:3. Can you think of other things the Bible says about us?

PRAYER

Dear God, thank you for loving me and designing every part of me. I am not wrong—I am exactly what you intended. Please help me accept more of your love every day, and to listen to what you say about me, not what others say. Amen.

WEEKS
35-39

TECHNOLOGY

My phone and me

> **"Use your worldly resources to benefit others and make friends. Then, when your possessions are gone, they will welcome you to an eternal home."**
>
> **LUKE 16:9**

Phones have many great qualities. They build friendships—we often get to know our friends better through messages and video calls. Apps help us develop new skills such as learning a language, keyboard skills, or stop-motion animation—and we can even download apps that help us get to know Jesus better. And games on a phone are fun, exercise our brain, and entertain us!

But phones can also become addictive. Apps are designed to keep us scrolling, keep us tapping. Too much phone use can be bad for our minds and bodies. It can cause anxiety, focus us on things that aren't healthy or true, and cause us to question our worth. It can take us away from real-life interaction, physical exercise, and time spent outdoors, as well as the present moment.

Jesus tells an interesting parable in Luke 16 about a shrewd manager. Jesus says we don't necessarily need to avoid possessions altogether, but instead learn to use them for the glory of God.

So, rather than think about what we can't wait to do on our phones, or worry about the impact it's having on our mental health, why not consider how our phones can help us honor God more? How can we use our phones to "benefit others" and "make friends"? Can we use technology to be generous and thoughtful, or to deepen friendships? Maybe we can even use technology to share something about Jesus with those we love, for example, by sharing Christian social media posts, or sending encouraging Bible verses to others.

CONVERSATION STARTERS

- If Jesus had a phone, what kinds of apps do you think he would download?
- What are the good things you do with your phone? Are there other good things you could use it for?
- Which aspects of phone use do you feel are more damaging? Which apps make it hard for you to stop using them? If you don't have a phone, how do you think others struggle with their phone use?
- Check out the full story in Luke 16:1–9. It's a strange parable, because Jesus seems to be praising the actions of a manager who's a little sneaky and dishonest. But what does Jesus say is "good" about his actions (v.8)?
- Now read on—Luke 16:10–13. How can you relate Jesus's wisdom to your phone and how you use it?

PRAYER

Dear Jesus, thank you for giving me technology to connect with the world around me. Please help me to use a phone responsibly and for your glory. Please don't let it take away from my relationship with you, and please give me the self-control to put it down when needed. Amen.

Speaking to others online

No one can tame the tongue. It is restless and evil . . . Sometimes it praises our Lord . . . and sometimes it curses those . . . made in the image of God.

JAMES 3:8A,9

My boys have a friend—let's call her Sarah—who was recently rejected by her two besties. They simply texted her saying, "We just don't want to be a three anymore," and that was that. Fortunately, Sarah has other friends who supported and included her when this happened—but not until after she felt extremely upset at the words of her friends.

It was a horrible situation, but we used it to remind our kids of the importance of how we speak to others online. One of the gifts God has given us when communicating with others is body language. When we speak to someone face-to-face, we automatically adjust our tone or language depending on how the other person is responding.

For example, if you jokingly poke fun at a friend, but their eyebrows rise, their cheeks go red, or their body stiffens up—you'll realize they didn't take it as a joke. You can then apologize and explain that you didn't mean to offend them.

However, the problem with *online* communication is that we can't see the other person's reactions. It becomes easier to speak harsh words when you can't see the upset you are causing. I'm pretty sure Sarah's friends wouldn't have been as blunt if they'd delivered that message face-to-face.

James is reminding us of how powerful our tongues are—for good or for bad. When we speak with others via technology, let's imagine they're sitting in front of us. Let's remember that God loves them deeply. Let's be kind, gentle, and encouraging with our words—online and offline.

CONVERSATION STARTERS

- Can you think of a time when someone's words praised or encouraged you? How did you feel?
- Can you think of a time when someone's words (online or offline) hurt or insulted you? How did they make you feel?
- Think about how Jesus spoke to people—if nothing comes to mind, flick through a gospel (Matthew, Mark, Luke, or John) to find his encounters with others. How many words can you think of that describe how Jesus spoke to others?
- Look up Proverbs 15:1–2. Have you ever known a situation where someone's harsh words led to a worse situation? How might it have been resolved sooner with kind or forgiving words?
- Read (and memorize, if you can) Proverbs 16:24. Think about the people close to you. How might your words be like "honey" to them?

PRAYER

Lord God, Please help me to make wise choices when I speak with others, especially online, where I can't see their reactions. Please protect me from the harsh words of others. Amen.

Taking control of screen time

So prepare your minds for action and exercise self-control. Put all your hope in the gracious salvation that will come to you when Jesus Christ is revealed to the world.

1 PETER 1:13

Have you ever spent a long time on your phone or another screen device and felt kinda yucky at the end? Like realizing how much of a time-suck that was? Or feeling like your life doesn't match up to the Insta perfection you've just witnessed?

The online world rarely represents real life. People show highlights, new outfits, fun trips, and clever pranks. They don't show the boring realities of homework, chores, bad hair days, and teeth-brushing.

It's not healthy to constantly compare our normal to everyone else's best. But it can also be really hard to step away from our phones when they're showing us lavish lifestyles or hilarious videos.

We need self-control, and Jesus's disciple Peter understood two important things about this fruit of the Spirit:

- Self-control involves us actively playing our part (*"prepare your minds for action"*). We have to make an active decision to put it down at sensible times.
- We can't do it on our own (*"Put all your hope in the gracious salvation"*). We're just not strong enough! When our own efforts fall short, that's when the Holy Spirit's power can help us honor God.

In fact, it is *as* we put our hope in Jesus that we will find ourselves being less tempted by the false "treasures" of this world. What Jesus offers us is far, far better than a Target haul or prank videos.

CONVERSATION STARTERS

- Can you relate to that yucky feeling of spending a long time glued to a screen? Be as specific as you can about what you felt and why.
- If Jesus was a kid with a phone today, what boundaries do you think he would put in place? When would he use his phone, and when would he lay it aside?
- What type of content most regularly draws you in, and why do you think it is so addictive?
- Self-control is a fruit of the Spirit. Look up all nine fruits in Galatians 5:22–23. Which other fruits are important when thinking about how we use our phones and devices?
- Read Hebrews 12:1–4. What kind of encouragement do these verses give as we try to become more controlled about our screen time? What tips does the writer give us?

PRAYER

Dear God, thank you for the screen-based entertainment I enjoy. Please give me self-control so I can enjoy screens in a healthy way. I don't want to become addicted to them and miss out on all the good things you have for me to experience and offer. Amen.

Not everything you read is true

"When the Spirit of truth comes, he will guide you into all truth."

JOHN 16:13A

My 10-year-old twins are about to have a room makeover. They are excitedly picking out paint colors and new furniture, and we go online together nearly every day to search for ideas.

The internet is amazing, isn't it? Whatever you're doing, you can always find inspiration, hacks, and tips.

However, we need to be careful because *anyone* can write things and put them on the internet. And this means that not everything we read is true.

It doesn't matter so much if my boys find terrible color ideas, or furniture with one-star reviews. We can just move on to another search result.

But there are others on the internet who will tell you how to live your life. Some of their suggestions might be wise, but some of it might be bad advice. How can we tell the difference?

Jesus says it is the Holy Spirit who leads us into all truth. His disciples didn't yet have the Holy Spirit, as it wasn't given until Jesus had gone back to heaven after his resurrection.

But for us today, we *do* have the Holy Spirit! So we can be confident that, as we chat with God and ask him questions about our lives, he will help us work out the right way to live—the way that honors him. Then it will be much easier to figure out whether what we read is true or not.

CONVERSATION STARTERS

- Can you think of something you've read online recently that doesn't seem true when matched up against God's word? (If not, open your phone/device now and see if you can find something!) What is God's truth in this scenario?
- Jesus never lies. What practical steps can you take to get to know him better?
- When you read something online, do you automatically assume it's true, or do you question it? What or who could help you decide whether it's true or not?
- Read John 8:31–36. What does sin do to us? By contrast, what is Jesus saying the truth does for us?
- Check out John 14:1–6. Look at Thomas' question. Sometimes we feel clueless about where our lives are going or how we should behave. What does Jesus's answer in verse 6 suggest we do?

PRAYER

Lord Jesus, there are so many voices around me in things I hear, watch, and read. I trust that you are the truth. So please help me figure out whether what I'm hearing is from you or not. Thank you that in your truth I am free! Amen.

WEEK 39

Responding to world events

> **Pray for all people. Ask God to help them; intercede on their behalf, and give thanks for them. Pray this way for kings and all . . . in authority.**
>
> 1 TIMOTHY 2:1–2A

One of the advantages of the digital world is the amount of news we receive and the speed at which it travels.

When I was growing up *(argh, sorry! Do you switch off when you hear your parents say this?!)* . . . well, I'm going to tell you anyway! When I was growing up, we only heard the news at certain times, when the TV played the news show.

Very important news got a "newsflash," when they'd break into whatever you were watching to say the Pope had died or something. But otherwise, we just didn't really hear the amount of news we hear today, and certainly not as quickly. It's not that things weren't happening; it's just that they didn't make it to our news.

Is it good or bad that we hear so much about the world today? Sure, it's good to be informed about what others are going through in different places. But it can also cause anxiety and fear. So how should we respond?

In today's reading, Paul is advising Timothy to pray for those in charge of the nations. We can do the same.

We might feel powerless when we hear about wars, famines, protests, or modern slavery. But God is not powerless. When we pray, we are expecting him to intervene to bring peace, provision, kindness, and dignity to all. Our fears diminish as we place them in the hands of the only one who can save the world and trust that "thy will be done."

CONVERSATION STARTERS

- Do you think it's important to know what's happening in the world? Why or why not?
- Think about a current news story that feels hopeless. What could you pray for those involved?
- Go to your local news website and read some news from your community. What and who could you pray for?
- Read Matthew 22:15–22. The Pharisees are trying to trick Jesus. How does his answer in verse 21 help us honor and pray for our leaders, even if we might not agree with them?
- Look at Psalm 72. Can you make a list of all the things that are prayed for, for the king? (It's a longer psalm, so if you don't have time, just look at the first five verses.)

PRAYER

Dear God, when I hear about horrible things happening in the world, I feel really sad. But I know you are able to perform miracles. Please, would you inspire the leaders of __________ (name a place in the news right now) to work together for peace and provision? Amen.

WEEKS
40-47

PUBERTY AND GROWING UP

My amazing body

You made all the delicate, inner parts of my body and knit me together in my mother's womb. Thank you for making me so wonderfully complex! Your workmanship is marvelous.

PSALM 139:13-14

How do you feel about your body? What kinds of clever things can it do?

Maybe your body enables you to run really fast, do a cartwheel, or swing from monkey bars. Perhaps your brain dreams up cool stories, works out math problems in a second, or remembers historical facts with ease. Maybe your hands create beautiful artwork or crafts.

Even if you have a disability that puts limits on what your body can do, your body is still amazing! It's keeping you alive by doing millions of clever tasks every day without you even thinking about them: breathing, digesting, fighting colds, healing cuts, creating neural pathways in your brain, and so much more.

Sadly, many people are unhappy with how their body looks or functions. It's not wrong to want to look our best, but hating our bodies or things we can't change about it can result in years of unhappiness, as people try to "fix" the bits they feel aren't right. Understanding that it was God himself who knit us together can help us learn to love the body he made for us.

Every small detail has been designed by him. Can you imagine God sitting at a drawing board, sketching you out, then standing back to admire his workmanship? "Ah, marvelous!" he says with a smile. "I love this person!"

Interestingly, today's verses focus not on our outward appearance, but on the "inner parts" of our bodies. Even when we're struggling to love what we look like outwardly, we can remember how brilliantly God has made our bodies to function on the inside.

CONVERSATION STARTERS

- How do you think Jesus might have looked?
- Which feature of your body's appearance or function do you appreciate the most?
- Read Luke 7:36–50. What assumptions did Simon make about the woman because of how she looked and behaved? What was Jesus's response?
- Check out 1 Samuel 16:6–7. Samuel thought God's next king would be the one whose body looked the strongest and fittest. God had made Eliab's body this way and wasn't rejecting him as a person, but he wasn't going to be the next king. Do you judge others by their appearances? What might help you not to do this?

PRAYER

Creator God, thank you for creating me and all the different people I see around me. There is such variety in how we all look and what we can do! Please help me to always remember that I am your workmanship, and to love my body as you do. Amen.

Hair . . . *where?*

> **For everything there is a season, a time for every activity under heaven.**
>
> ECCLESIASTES 3:1

Some pretty crazy stuff starts to happen during puberty—like hair starting to grow in places you've never had hair before!

It can all seem a bit embarrassing and weird—but did you know that this hair is there for a reason? It's catching sweat and bacteria, keeping everything clean and healthy. God isn't embarrassed by hair—he made it for good reasons.

Every part of our bodies has been designed to work beautifully by our wonderfully creative Father God. (Even when some parts don't work as they should, we can still marvel at the design work God has put in to enable us to do what we *can* do.)

Some of the changes we experience in our bodies and minds during puberty might feel confusing or even unwelcome, but the writer of Ecclesiastes reminds us here that God has set a season for everything. Puberty allows our bodies to grow into adult bodies, which will be capable of doing things a child's body isn't designed for. Puberty is a *good* thing!

It may feel a little awkward to talk to your parents about what you're experiencing, but remember, they've been through this, too, so they understand and will likely have great advice on how to manage these changes.

And you can talk to God about it. After all, it is God who has designed your body this way.

CONVERSATION STARTERS

- How do you think Jesus might have dealt with puberty? Is there anything about puberty that you're not looking forward to? If so, why? Can you chat through your concerns with a trusted grown-up?
- How do you feel about the fact that God has designed puberty? Can you see reasons for the changes that have happened or will happen?
- Other mammals reach full maturity much sooner than humans. Why do you think God designed humans to take longer to develop into adults? And what do you think are the benefits of having many years of childhood?
- Read the full passage in Ecclesiastes 3:1–8. Which lines stand out to you? Which ones can you relate to?

PRAYER

Dear God, I'm excited about growing up, but I'm also a bit nervous. Thank you for creating my body to grow and change in all the right ways. Please help me to cling to this belief when I'm feeling unsure about the changes. I trust that your design is amazing. Amen.

But I want to stay a kid!

> **When I was a child, I spoke and thought and reasoned as a child. But when I grew up, I put away childish things.**
>
> 1 CORINTHIANS 13:11

How do you feel about birthdays? Are you excited to reach the next age—or sad to leave an age you'll never be again?

Sometimes a new age brings with it new privileges—like a later bedtime, a higher allowance, or being allowed to go out with friends. But with these privileges come responsibilities, such as making sure you get enough sleep, budgeting your money, or staying safe when there are no adults around.

There might be times when you think, *I don't want all this responsibility! I liked it better when I was able to play without having to worry about anything else!* Let's zoom out a little to discover the importance of growing up.

1 Corinthians 13 is about love. Paul says love will last forever, unlike prophecy and other spiritual gifts that the Corinthians thought were the most important things. These gifts are only for a season. Once we get to live with Jesus forever in heaven, we won't need them anymore, because we'll get to chat with Jesus all the time! But love will always be important.

In today's verse, Paul says that these spiritual gifts are like being a child—incredibly helpful, but not forever. It would be pretty weird if children never grew up! While childhood can be wonderful, its aim is to help us grow into adults. Childhood helps us grow skills and character that we'll use throughout life.

We don't need to be worried about growing up. God is with us and will help us as we gradually take on responsibilities and new independence. And we can always have fun—we call that "our inner child!"

CONVERSATION STARTERS

- How do you think Jesus felt about growing up? Do you think he was excited about all he'd get to do, or nervous about having that responsibility?
- What do you enjoy about life at your age? How do you think that will be different when you grow up?
- What do you *not* enjoy about life now? How do you think this will be better when you grow up?
- Read 1 Samuel 3:15–21. God has given Samuel a challenging prophetic word to pass on to Eli the priest. How is God helping Samuel grow up well? (Verse 19 is key!)
- Check out Psalm 18:1–2. How does this verse encourage you as you think about growing up? You could underline words and phrases that stand out to you.

PRAYER

Lord God, I am so excited to get older and have more independence and freedom, but this can sometimes feel a little scary, too. Please remind me that you are always with me, my strength and protection, and that I can always talk to you about anything. Amen.

Starting to change

Jesus grew in wisdom and in stature and in favor with God and all the people.

LUKE 2:52

We don't know very much about Jesus's childhood, but we do have one story:

Jesus was 12. His parents were on their way back from the Passover festival when they realized Jesus wasn't with them. They thought he was somewhere in the traveling crowd, but he was actually back in the temple, listening to the Jewish teachers and asking questions.

Today's verse occurs just after this story. It is a very short summary of what happened to Jesus between the ages of 12 and 30! But it teaches us two important things about growing up.

First, we learn the importance of growing both "in wisdom and in stature [height]." Jesus was getting taller, and his voice would have changed just like any teenage boy. But alongside this, he grew in "wisdom." He took every opportunity (like in the temple at age 12) to learn from others. As we grow toward adulthood, are we wanting to grow in wisdom, too?

Second, we learn that Jesus grew in favor with "God and all the people." It's wonderful when we get to know God and learn to live for him. But it's also important to grow in favor with other people.

Of course, there will always be people who don't like us—that's on them, not us. But we can ask the Holy Spirit to fill us with kindness, goodness, and integrity so that we become the sort of people others warm up to.

CONVERSATION STARTERS

- Who are the people in your life you consider to be wise? How could you learn from them?
- Why do you think Jesus grew in favor with other people? What was it about him that others appreciated?
- Which qualities do you have that make others warm up to you? Thank God for giving them to you!
- Which qualities would you like to have more of? (You could check Galatians 5:22–23 for ideas.) Ask the Holy Spirit to grow these in you.
- Find 1 Timothy 4:12. Timothy was a young leader. How does Paul encourage him to live? You might like to memorize this verse if it encourages you.

PRAYER

Dear Jesus, thank you that you know what it's like to grow up. As I grow in height, please help me to also grow in wisdom. Put people around me I can learn from and ask questions of. Make me the kind of person others can trust. Amen.

Feeling out of control

> **God is our refuge and strength, always ready to help in times of trouble. So we will not fear when earthquakes come and the mountains crumble into the sea.**
>
> PSALM 46:1-2

With all the changes happening to our bodies, we can sometimes feel a little out of control and anxious. It can feel like our bodies are taking on a life of their own, and we can do nothing to stop or slow down the changes.

The psalmist of Psalm 46 is saying that even if the worst happens—earthquakes and landslides—we are able to live without fear, because God is on our side. The challenges of puberty are nowhere near these natural disasters in terms of seriousness, and yet they can feel very real and fear-inducing when we're going through them.

In times of worry, this psalm reminds us that God is:

- Our refuge—a place we can hide when we're afraid, a place that offers protection and safety for us
- Our strength—when we are not feeling strong or brave
- Always ready to help in times of trouble—we can talk to him anytime of the day or night about anything at all. He's always there, and always listening.

Can I talk to God about my body? Yes, you can! God knows what you're going through, and he knows that growing up is not always easy or comfortable. As you bring your concerns to him, you will find him to be a safe place, a source of strength, and an empathetic listener.

CONVERSATION STARTERS

- What parts of puberty are you finding (or expecting to be) challenging, painful, or awkward? Tell God about them.
- Is there anything about puberty that you feel unprepared for? What might help you feel more reassured?
- How does it encourage you to know that Jesus went through puberty?
- Check out Psalm 34:1–7. What does this psalm say that God gives us, takes away, or does for us when we pray to him (verses 4–7)?
- Read Isaiah 61:1–7. Maybe you don't consider yourself "poor," "broken-hearted," or "oppressed", but we serve a God who comes alongside us even when we're feeling a little embarrassed or in pain. How can these verses encourage us when we feel out of control?

PRAYER

Dear Lord, you have created my body to develop and grow in this way, and I thank you for that, even though sometimes it may be embarrassing, painful, or just plain weird. Please help me to remember I can call out to you about anything at all, no matter how I'm feeling. Amen.

When my body doesn't look how I want it to look

> You watched me as I was being formed in utter seclusion, as I was woven together in the dark of the womb. You saw me before I was born.
>
> PSALM 139:15–16A

Have you ever looked around a crowded place and marveled at the variety of body shapes and sizes? We have a very creative God who has designed so many different human beings!

We know, though, that lots of people are unhappy with the way they look. The beauty industry is worth billions of dollars—this means the billions of dollars people spend to change or "improve" their appearance. Whether it's expensive products, hair extensions, acrylic nails, fillers, or cosmetic surgery, it seems that the human race is on a constant mission to make themselves look different.

As our bodies are changing, we might not like the way they look. This might be because certain parts of our body grow quicker than others. We might grow really tall before we develop muscle and tone—or we might fill out before we have the height to match.

But however much we might dislike our bodies, God absolutely adores them! He loves how he has made each one of us. He knew our appearance even before our parents did. He wove us together in the womb and delighted in each and every detail of how we look.

There is nothing wrong with the way you look! As your body changes and develops, there might be seasons where you find it easier or harder to love yourself. But always remember: You are the craftsmanship of the Master Designer. He has designed you to look this way and develop this way, and he loves every bit of you.

CONVERSATION STARTERS

- How do you think Jesus might have felt about his body when he was growing up?
- How do you feel about your body right now? Which is your favorite feature? Which is your least favorite?
- Why do you think people spend so much money on altering their appearance? What do you think God wants them to know?
- Look up Isaiah 53:2–3, which is a prophecy about Jesus. What does it say about his appearance? Does this description surprise you? Why/why not?
- Check out 1 Peter 3:3–4. What's more important than the time, energy, and money we might pour into our appearance? How could we develop this other part of us?

PRAYER

Dear God, when I am tempted to reject the body you have given me, please help me learn to love it. As it changes and develops, please draw close to me and remind me that these changes are good changes. Thank you. Amen.

There's no one quite like me

> **"And the very hairs on your head are all numbered. So don't be afraid; you are more valuable to God than a whole flock of sparrows."**
>
> LUKE 12:7

As we go through life, our bodies are constantly changing. It's totally normal to go through seasons of liking the way you look, and seasons of not liking it.

You might wish parts of you were bigger and more developed—or other parts of you weren't quite so developed. You might be dissatisfied with your height, your hair thickness, your skin type, or any other physical feature. You might struggle with acne and wonder why you get breakouts so easily when others seem to avoid them.

But do you know what? Today's verse reminds you that you are valuable to God and deeply loved by him. He knows every detail of you—even the number of hairs on your head—because he designed you this way. He also knows exactly how and when puberty will change your body. He loves how you look, and he's not waiting till you're fully grown to love your appearance—he loves it right now!

This truth won't necessarily change how you feel about your appearance overnight, but dwelling on it over time will help you grow to love your body if you don't already do so.

If you're craving someone else's body shape, hair color, or flawless skin right now, it might help to remember that God didn't create you to be *that* person. Just as there are things you might envy about how they look, guess what? There are qualities and traits you have that this person doesn't. Who knows, they might secretly be envying *you*!

CONVERSATION STARTERS

- If you could change your body in one way, what would you do and why? What might it take for you to learn to love this part of you more?
- When you see celebrities on social media, YouTube, or TV, why do you think they look so perfect? Is this attainable for most people? Is it even real? Why or why not?
- How do you feel about the truth that God knows every intimate detail about you, like the hairs on your head? What does this attention to detail teach you?
- There is no one quite like you! Does this encourage you or make you anxious, or a bit of both, or something else? Why?
- Look up a story where Jesus healed or encouraged someone who didn't think much of themselves or their appearance. (You could try Matthew 8:1–4, Luke 19:1–10, or John 4:1–26.) What does Jesus's compassion teach you about judging by appearances?

PRAYER

Dear Lord, you have created me to be unique, and I am so grateful, even though sometimes I find it hard to love how I look. Please show me how you see me, so I can learn to love the way you've made me to be. Amen.

WEEK 47

Learning to respect myself

> **What are mere mortals that you should think about them, human beings that you should care for them? Yet you made them only a little lower than God and crowned them with glory and honor.**
>
> PSALM 8:4-5

When others disrespect us, it's easy to lose respect for ourselves. But when we learn to respect ourselves, it becomes easier to stand up against others' disrespectful treatment of us.

This psalm sets a foundation in place for self-respect. God could have made us as minions—mindless slaves just doing what we're told. But he didn't! He made us "only a little lower than God"—wow! We don't deserve this kind of status, and yet God has lavished it on us. Who are other people to disrespect us when God himself has crowned us with "glory and honor"?

Your body is God's beautiful, treasured design, and no one has the right to disrespect it by doing something against your consent. Sometimes the bad behavior of others against us can make us feel icky—like we're somehow "used" or "unclean."

But this is not how Jesus sees us. It is the person who has disrespected us who is unclean—not us. They need to take their sin to Jesus to be made right with God—we can't do that for them.

What we can do is tell a trusted grown-up what happened, set boundaries together for the person in question, and ask for God's help to forgive them. It may not be a quick or easy process—just never forget that your worth is set by God, not the actions or opinions of others. Respect yourself as God respects you—then it will become easier to recognize, and rise above, others' disrespect.

CONVERSATION STARTERS

- How did Jesus show respect for others in his words and actions? Is this how you treat others? Why or why not?
- Why do you think some people don't respect others' bodies? What do you think they believe about others and/or themselves?
- Have you ever been in a situation where someone's actions toward you made you feel uncomfortable? What did you do?
- What is your response to the fact that God has crowned you with "glory and honor" and made you only a little lower than himself? How does this make you feel?
- King David messed up big time with a woman who was married to someone else. He disrespected her and her husband (see 2 Samuel 11). Check out 2 Samuel 12:1–13, when God sent the prophet Nathan to confront David. What does this passage teach you about what God thinks about the sin of disrespecting someone's body?

PRAYER

Lord God, you have made us in a way that we are only a little lower than you. That is amazing! Please help me to honor and respect others' bodies, remembering that they're your children. And please protect me from others' disrespect, too. Amen.

WEEKS
48-52

MONEY AND INDEPENDENCE

WEEK 48

Managing my allowance

Don't love money; be satisfied with what you have. For God has said, "I will never fail you. I will never abandon you."

HEBREWS 13:5

Do you get a regular allowance, or will you when you're older? Do you occasionally get gifts of money from family or friends?

However much we have, or however frequently we receive it, good money management is a really important life skill. We can start learning it now as we deal in small amounts, but we will continue to learn in adulthood when our income and expenses grow much bigger.

One of the main reasons why people overspend and get into debt is because they want lots of nice things they can't afford. Instead of saving up for a fun trip, a new car, or a house renovation, they use credit cards and loans to get those things *now*. But then they end up paying *more* for them, because those cards and loans charge interest (extra money you pay for the privilege of borrowing it in the first place).

We are given brilliant wisdom in today's reading, which will help us avoid overspending. *Don't love money; be satisfied with what you have*. That's hard! It's not easy seeing our friends in amazing outfits or with brand-new tech when we can't afford those things ourselves.

But what does the Bible go on to say? That God will *never fail us or abandon us*. He will make sure we have everything we need—including his presence. God is worth much more than new clothes, which won't look as fashionable in a few months, or swanky gadgets, which lose their novelty appeal pretty quickly.

CONVERSATION STARTERS

- Are you a saver or a spender? Do you always have money in your wallet, or do you spend it as soon as you get it?
- What kinds of things would you buy if your allowance was *tripled*? Are these things you need? Do you think you would make good use of them?
- What do you think Jesus might have spent his allowance on?
- Look up 1 Timothy 6:6–8. What do you think of these verses? Do you agree? Why/why not? Does it change your attitude about money?
- Continue to read 1 Timothy 6:9–10. What kinds of trouble might rich people get into because of their money?

PRAYER

Dear God, thank you for the money you give me through other people. Please help me to learn to manage it well by being content with what I have so I'm not tempted to overspend. Please make me satisfied with your presence, so I don't crave things I don't need. Amen.

Being a cheerful giver

You must each decide in your heart how much to give. And don't give reluctantly or in response to pressure. "For God loves a person who gives cheerfully."

2 CORINTHIANS 9:7

There are three things we can do with our money: spend it, save it, and give it. Good money management includes all three.

Today, we're focusing on giving. This verse talks about money, but we could also include our possessions, time, and talents.

Whatever we give, Paul is clear: We must not do so just because we think we should. God doesn't want us to be resentful about what we give. He wants us to give cheerfully!

How can we be cheerful about giving our money or possessions away?

One answer comes in the following verse, which says God will *generously provide* for all we need. So if we're reluctant to give because we're worried we won't have enough for ourselves, we can relax—God will make sure we have enough.

Another answer comes in the faces of those we give to. When we buy candy for our friend who hasn't got any money, or put a couple of dollars in the offering at church, we may see the recipient's face light up in gratitude. This gives us all the warm, fuzzy feelings of knowing we have provided for someone else's need!

(If you're still not convinced, try to remember how *you've* felt in the past when people have given you things.)

And a final answer: Giving to others shapes our character. Through our giving, God loosens our grip on money, helping us to find fulfillment in him rather than endlessly chasing wealth, which never truly satisfies.

CONVERSATION STARTERS

- Can you remember a time when someone gave you something you really needed or wanted? How did it feel?
- Can you remember a time when you gave something to someone who was grateful? What did it cost you? How did it bless them?
- Read John 6:1–15. Jesus was given something small, but he multiplied it to provide for thousands of people. Do you think he still multiplies our generosity today? How does this make you feel?
- Focus on the boy in John 6:1–15. We don't know how much he ate, but we do know that there was more left over than what he had given. What does this teach us about God's provision?
- Check out Mark 12:41–44. What does Jesus say about the widow? How do you feel about this?

PRAYER

Dear Jesus, sometimes I find it really difficult to give away what I have, because I'm worried about not having enough. But throughout the Bible, I can see that you always provide what we need when we need it. Please help me to trust you and give cheerfully. Amen.

Saving for the future

Tell them to use their money to do good . . . By doing this they will be storing up their treasure as a good foundation for the future.

1 TIMOTHY 6:18A,19

Saving our money can be a really positive thing to do. It means we can buy bigger items eventually, or put away funds for something in the future, like going to college.

In today's verse, Paul is speaking to Timothy about those who are "rich in this world." That's us! You might not feel very rich, but if your parents are earning money, you have a roof over your head, food to eat, clothes to wear, and you *still* have some money left over, you are much richer than most of the world's population.

The world tells us to save for our earthly future—a future that may involve learning to drive, continuing our education, buying a house, or starting a family. But God tells us that if we really want a "good foundation for the future," we will invest in the things that grow his kingdom—our heavenly future. There is a lot of need in the world. God's plan is for us to share what we have so that no one goes without.

If you are able to save, God might use some of that money for your future needs. But he might also invite you to give to others who need clean water, food, education, healthcare, or to hear the good news of Jesus Christ.

CONVERSATION STARTERS

- Are you a natural saver? Do you hoard money away, or do you spend it before it's able to build up?
- What might help you to save? Setting aside a percentage of your allowance? Starting a savings or investment account and asking your parents to transfer a little of your allowance there before it comes to you?
- Read the parable of the rich fool in Luke 12:13–21. What mistake did he make? How do people hoard their money today in similar ways?
- Ask Jesus what he thinks you could do with your money to grow the kingdom of heaven here on earth.
- Check out 1 Peter 1:4–6. Inheritance is the money and other items you might receive when a loved one dies. How is our heavenly inheritance far better than any inheritance we might receive on earth?

PRAYER

Lord God, you have been so generous to me, and I ask you to help me manage my money well. Please, would you help me to save sensibly, and then show me how to use my savings so that your kingdom grows? I know you will provide all my needs. Amen.

Not enough hours in the day?

So be careful how you live. Don't live like fools, but like those who are wise. Make the most of every opportunity in these evil days.

EPHESIANS 5:15-16

Do you sometimes wish you had more time to do everything you want to do? Do you run out of time for the things you need to do?

As we grow older, we become busier. Schoolwork ramps up as we head toward bigger projects and exams. We might find ourselves spending more time going out with our friends. And there are still chores to be done at home, family to see, and teeth to clean!

It can feel like a lot. But Paul has encouraging words for us when it comes to how we use our time. Yes, it is possible to waste time ("live like fools"), but Paul urges us to live like those who are "wise," being careful, and making the most of opportunities.

What does this look like?

Well, to start with, we can ask ourselves what opportunities God has given us. The opportunity to be educated? Then work hard and do your best. The opportunity to grow up in a family? Enjoy time with them. The opportunity to have friends? Invest in these relationships by spending time with them.

Think about other opportunities God has given you, and how you might make the most of them.

Other stuff can fit in around these opportunities—looking after ourselves, doing chores, relaxing.

There are only 24 hours in each day, many of which are needed for sleeping. So we can't do *everything*. If we don't feel we have enough hours, we can ask ourselves, *What needs to go?*

CONVERSATION STARTERS

- What opportunities has God given you in your life? How can you make the most of them?
- If time management is hard right now, ask yourself: *What am I doing that's less important?* You could make a list of things you *do* want to do, and refer back to it each day.
- How did Jesus spend his time? (Try to go beyond the obvious answers of teaching and healing! Flick through a gospel if you're not sure.)
- Read Psalm 127:2. If we're overly busy, we're likely to cut back on sleep. What does God say about that in this verse?
- Look up Psalm 90:12. None of us know how long we have here on earth. How does this change your perspective about how to live today?

PRAYER

Father God, thank you for giving me 24 hours in each day, and lots of fun things to do in that time. Please help me work out what is important to focus on and what needs to go. I don't want to waste my time on things that aren't from you. Amen.

Making good decisions

We can make our own plans, but the Lord gives the right answer . . . Commit your actions to the Lord, and your plans will succeed.

PROVERBS 16:1,3

Do you like making decisions? When you're choosing a pizza or movie, are you first to state your preference, or would you rather let your friend choose?

Some decisions aren't very important. Others can affect your whole life. That can feel a bit scary! When you were young, your parents likely made most decisions for you. But as you get older, you'll get more say in what you do and where you go.

How do we know which subjects to choose at school? What to study at college? Which jobs to go for? Who to go out with—and, later, whether to marry them?

These can all feel like really big decisions—and they are. But as Christians, we don't need to worry about them. We have a relationship with the all-knowing King of the Universe! We can talk to him anytime we like, asking him to guide us. We're never alone in our decision-making unless we choose to be.

God always knows the right thing to do. He can make our plans succeed too—but there's a condition to this. Did you spot it? "Commit your actions to the Lord." That means we need to be willing to bring our opportunities to him first.

God can't give us success in things that are against his nature. If we really want to do something that will bring harm to another person or to us, that's when God will gently steer us away from that option, toward a better path.

CONVERSATION STARTERS

- Do you have any big decisions to make right now? Why not ask Jesus to guide you as you think through the options?
- What kinds of big decisions will you need to make in the future? What might you find hard about this process?
- The Bible is full of stories of God guiding people—from Moses leading the Israelites out of Egypt (Exodus 3:7–10) to Ruth accompanying her mother-in-law to Bethlehem (Ruth 1:11–18) to Philip ministering to the Ethiopian (Acts 8:26–29). Look up one of these stories. What was the result of this person obeying God?
- Read Proverbs 3:5–6. You might like to memorize these verses. How do they challenge you? How do they encourage you?
- Check out James 4:13–15. How might you apply this message to your approach to the future?

PRAYER

Dear God, I thank you for all the amazing opportunities you have put in my life and even in the future I can't yet see. At every step, I want to walk with you, because I know your way is best. Please guide me clearly so I can make good decisions. Amen.

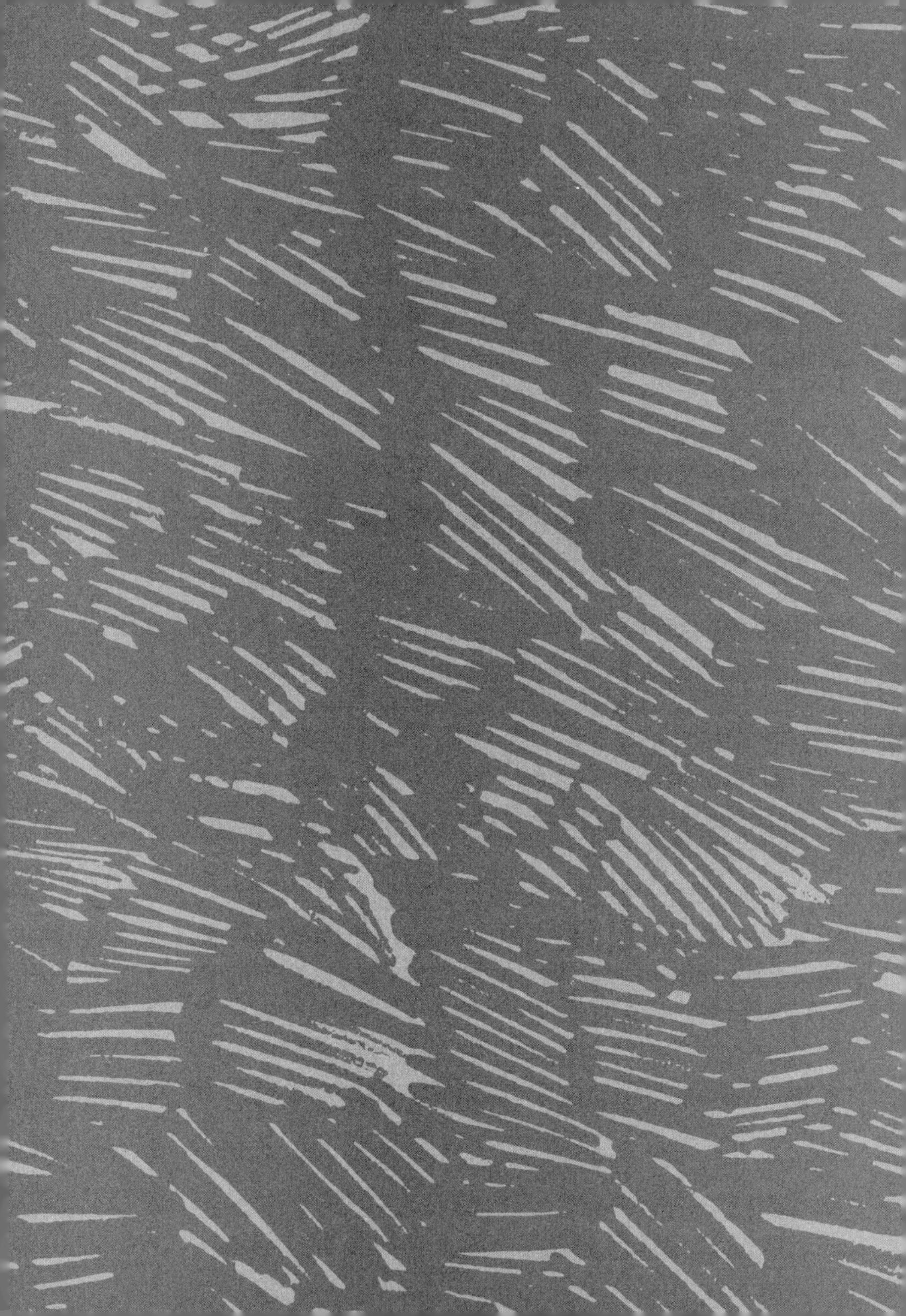

ACKNOWLEDGMENTS

If you have picked up this book, thank you. Thank you to your kids for being open to learning how God might want to speak into their lives. And thank you to *you*—parents, grandparents, caregivers—for investing in your child's life and faith journey. I hope this book encourages you in yours, too.

A huge thank you to Tahra, Kim, Bethany, Erica, Natalie, Patty, and the entire Zeitgeist team for recognizing the need for a book like this and bringing it to life. Thank you for allowing me to be a part of it. Your vision has been inspiring, and your feedback invaluable.

Thank you to Kristen Miele (Sex Ed Reclaimed) and Rachel Newham, whose expertise in sex education and mental health respectively, was so much appreciated when writing the 'Puberty and growing up' and 'Mental and emotional health' sections. Thank you for your wise comments and suggestions.

A huge thank you to my kids, who have been the inspiration for how and what I've written in these pages. At the time of this writing, two have passed through the preteen period, and two are in the trenches. This book draws on the experiences I've had parenting all four of you.

Thank you to Al, my equal partner in the daily joys and challenges of raising humans. From insane weekly scheduling to pondering how we can nurture who God has created our kiddoes to be, I'm so grateful to be parenting with you in the tiny details and the big picture.

Most of all, thank you to Jesus for enabling me to write this book and for reminding me just how much wisdom is contained within the Bible—for all of life. We parents need never be anxious about our kids growing up when we have God's word to guide us.

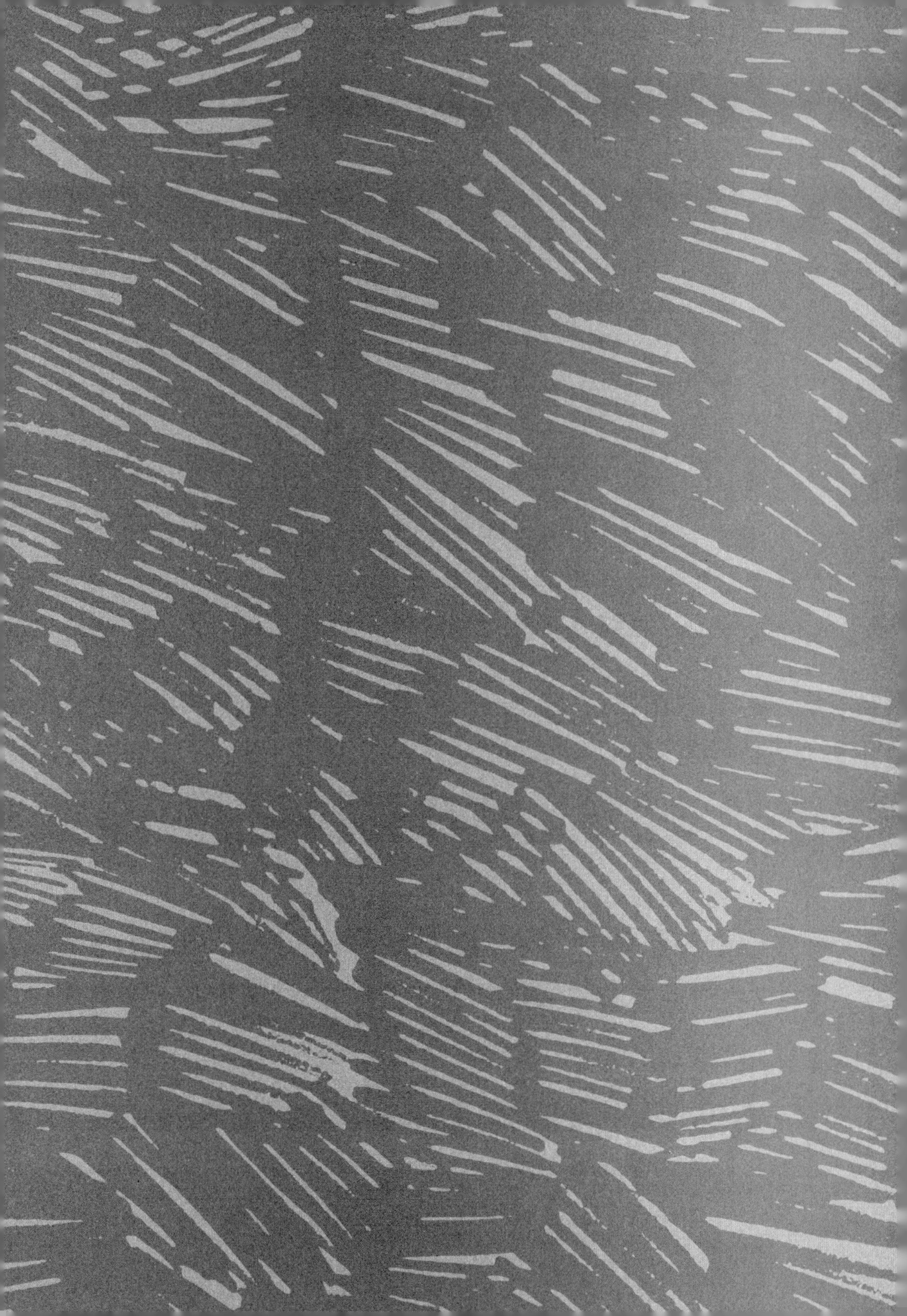

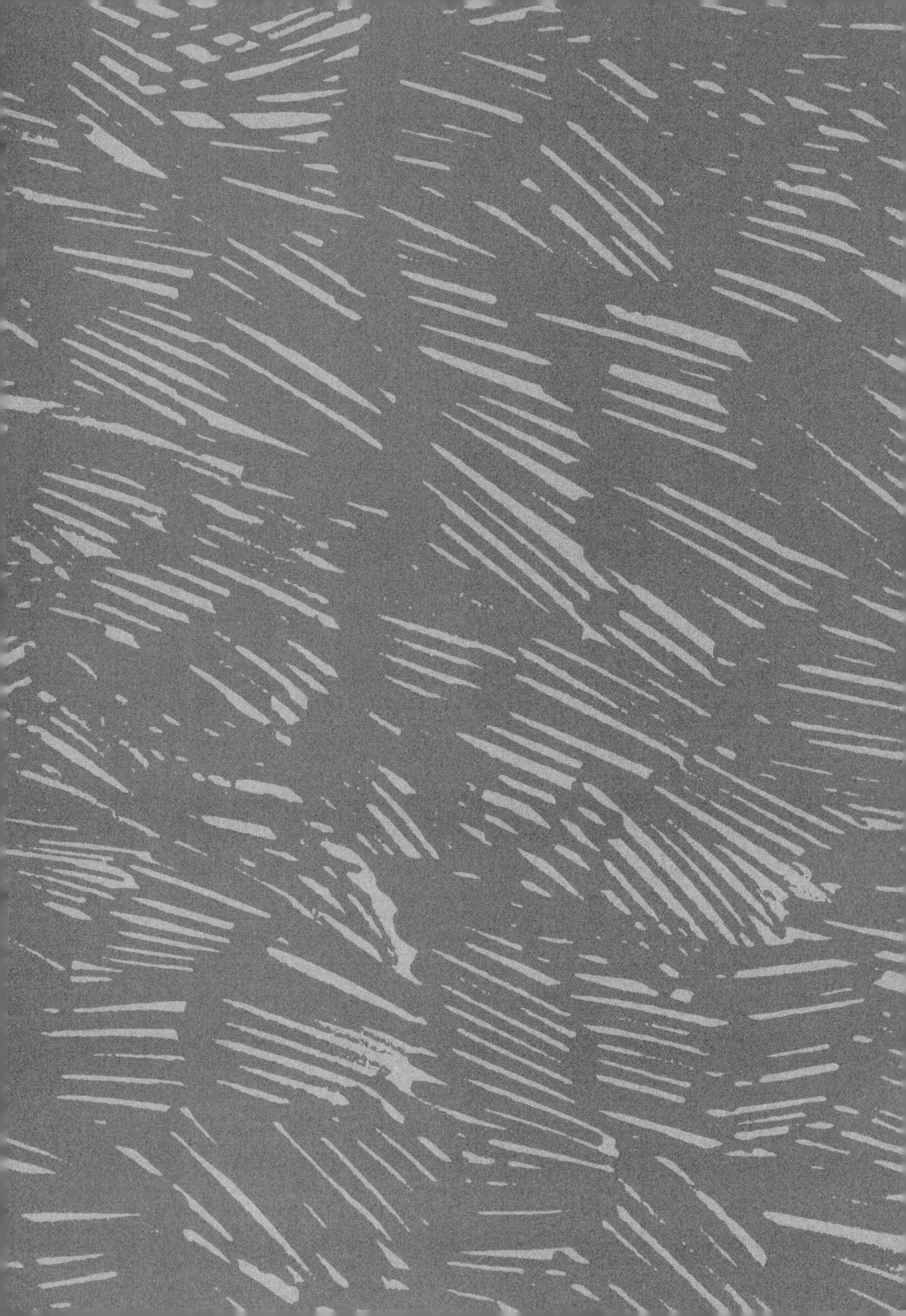

ABOUT THE AUTHOR

Lucy Rycroft is mom to four children ages 11 to 16, who arrived through both birth and adoption. She's married to Al, a church leader in beautiful York, England, where they make their home with their kids and their crazy cockapoo called Monty.

Lucy is the founder of The Hope-Filled Family, a ministry encouraging Christian parents, carers, and all those investing in the younger generation. She is the author of several books for adults and children, including *Busy Family Devotional* and the *Mighty Girl, Mighty God* series, which teaches younger children the fabulous stories of the female Bible heroes in beautiful rhyme (hers) and vibrant illustrations (not hers).

Lucy recently returned part-time to the classroom, her career prior to having kids, where she teaches music to 11-to-18-year-olds.

Parents, you can follow Lucy on Instagram @thehopefilledfamily for daily encouragement, or sign up for friendly Friday emails on her website, thehopefilledfamily.com.

Hi, parents and caregivers,

We hope you and your child enjoyed *What Would Jesus Do?* If you have any questions or concerns about this book, or have received a damaged copy, please contact customerservice@penguinrandomhouse.com. We're here and happy to help.

Also, please consider writing a review on your favorite retailer's website to let others know what you and your child thought of the book!

Sincerely,
The Zeitgeist Team